Plays of
Exploration and Discovery
for Grades 4–6

A Smith and Kraus Book
Published by Smith and Kraus, Inc.
PO Box 127, Lyme, NH 03768

First Edition: July 1999
10 9 8 7 6 5 4 3 2 1

Book design by Julia Hill Gignoux, Freedom Hill Design

The Library of Congress Cataloging-In-Publication Data
McCullough, L.E.
Plays of exploration and discovery, grades 4–6 / by L.E. McCullough.
p. cm. — (Young actors series)
Summary: Presents twelve original plays that depict important moments of discovery in science and geography by such people as Copernicus, Marie Curie, Benjamin Franklin, Amerigo Vespucci, and Florence Nightingale.
ISBN 1-57525-113-2
1. Explorers Juvenile drama. 2. Scientists Juvenile drama. 3. Children's plays, American. [1. Scientists Drama. 2. Explorers Drama. 3. Plays.]
I. Title. II. Series: Young actors series.
PS3563.C35297P5855   1999
812'.54—dc21   99-30020
CIP

Plays of
Exploration and Discovery
for Grades 4–6

L.E. McCullough

YOUNG ACTORS SERIES

A Smith and Kraus Book

This book is dedicated to my parents
and to the inspiration and counsel of
Madame Suzanne de la Croix,
scientist, musician, true believer.

Contents

Acknowledgments

Some individuals who have assisted in my various voyages of exploration and discovery: Victoria Calvert Kappel of HealthWorks Theatre, Chicago; Jessica Weiner of the IUPUI A.C.T.–OUT Ensemble, Indianapolis; Jane Rulon of the Indiana Film Commission; Jeffrey Sparks of the New Harmony Project; Anya Peterson Royce, Dept. of Anthropology, Indiana University; Eadie Barrie, Indiana Historical Society; Jay Brill of the Downtown Kiwanis Club; Frank Gillis of the Indiana University Archives of Traditional Music; Tim Sullivan; and Dave McCumisky, Music Sales, Inc.

Foreword

The important thing is not to stop questioning. Curiosity has its own reason for existing. One cannot help but be in awe when he contemplates the mysteries of eternity, of life, of the marvelous structure of reality.
— Albert Einstein, scientist

How reconcile this world of fact with the bright world of my imagining?
— Helen Keller, writer

The twelve plays in this book pay tribute to the courageous men and women throughout the ages who have used their imaginations to change our world for the better. Often these pioneer thinkers faced the scorn of colleagues, ridicule by the public, and even active opposition and persecution from civil, military, and religious authorities. Despite these obstacles, they persevered with their intuitive belief in the necessity to always question the status quo, always seek a new perspective, always strive to use the inherent power of the human mind to benefit the lot of all humanity.

These plays span a wide spectrum of subject and complexity, from simple dramatizations of great moments in scientific history and biographical surveys of notable discoverers to overviews of the history of science itself. *Plays of Exploration and Discovery* is a perfect class complement to any elementary/middle school science program and can serve as a starting point for discussion about the scientific process and basic scientific concepts, science vocabulary, the skills and training needed to be a scientist or explorer and even the re-creation of classic experiments.

Plays of Exploration and Discovery has been designed to combine with studies in other disciplines: history, language, dance, music, social studies, mathematics, etc. *Around the World with Nellie Bly* can be used with literature or journalism classes. *Mothers and Daughters of Invention* works well with units on women's history. *Everyday Science in Ben Franklin's America* and *"Lady of the Lamp": Florence Nightingale, Founder of Modern Nursing* integrate with history curriculum. *Counting, from Quipu to Googol* can supplement lesson plans in math.

Feel free to decorate the set with architecture, plants and art objects specific to the time period and culture. Ask a music teacher to add songs and music to any of the plays; go ahead and make it a class project by organizing a chorus or having students select appropriate recordings of music and songs to play before and after the performance. If you want to introduce more detailed biographical or costume information into your presentation of the plays, consult your school or local library for books and videos that will enhance your group's playmaking.

Besides those children enrolled in the onstage cast, others can be included in the production as lighting and sound technicians, prop masters, script coaches and stage managers. *Plays of Exploration and Discovery* is an excellent vehicle for getting other members of the school and community involved in your project. There are undoubtedly knowledgeable science workers and teachers in your area who can add interesting stories about their jobs. Try utilizing the talents of local school or youth orchestra members to play incidental music…get the school art club to paint scrims and backdrops… see if a senior citizens' group might volunteer time to sew costumes…inquire whether any local businesses might bring posters, brochures or samples of their products.

Most of all, have lots of fun. Realizing that many performing groups may have limited technical and space resources, I have kept sets, costumes and props minimal. However, if you do have the ability to fashion a facsimile 16th-century ocean vessel for *Naming the Unnamed: The Strange Saga of Amerigo Vespucci* or build a replica observatory for *"Constellations Then Arise": Astronomy in the Age of Copernicus* — go for it! Adding more music and dance and visual arts and crafts into the production involves more children and makes your play a genuinely multi-media event.

Similarly, I have supplied only basic stage and lighting directions.

Blocking is really the province of the director; once you get the play up and moving, feel free to suit cast and action to your available population and experience level of actors. When figuring out how to stage these plays, I suggest you follow the venerable UYI Method — Use Your Imagination. If the play calls for a boat, bring in a wood frame, an old bathtub or have children draw a boat and hang as a scrim behind where the actors perform. Keep in mind the spirit of the old Andy Hardy musicals: "C'mon, everybody! Let's make a show!"

Age and gender. Obviously, your purpose in putting on the play is to entertain as well as educate; even though one typically thinks of castle guards and king's soldiers as being male, there is no reason these roles can't be played in *your* production by females. After all, the essence of the theatrical experience is to suspend us in time and ask us to believe that anything may be possible. Once again, UYI! Adult characters can certainly be played by children costumed or made up to fit the part as closely as possible, or they can actually be played by adults. While the plays in *Plays of Exploration and Discovery* are intended to be performed chiefly by children, moderate adult involvement will add validation and let children know this isn't just a time-killing "kid project." If you want to get very highly choreographed or musically intensive, you will probably find a strategically placed onstage adult or two very helpful in keeping things moving smoothly. Still, *never* underestimate the capacity for even the youngest children to amaze you with their skill and ingenuity in making a show blossom.

Plays of Exploration and Discovery is a great way to enliven a child's love of learning and to set them on course for the day when he or she joyfully realizes (with the Renaissance philosopher Francis Bacon) that "Nam et ipsa scoentia potestas est" — *knowledge itself is power.*

L.E. McCullough, Ph.D.
Humanities Theatre Group
Indiana University-Purdue
University at Indianapolis
Indianapolis, Indiana

Mothers and Daughters of Invention:

4,000 Years of Women in Science

Until very recently, in most societies women were not permitted much chance to engage in scientific research, nor were they often given credit for the research they did conduct. Yet, throughout recorded history, women have been responsible for many important scientific discoveries and have devised numerous practical inventions to make our world a safer, healthier, happier place to live. Today, opportunities for women to excel in science and mathematics are greater than ever and will continue to grow in the future. As the saying goes, women not only "hold up half the sky," they are in the vanguard of exploring and transforming that sky.

RUNNING TIME: 20 minutes

TIME: Yesterday during study period

PLACE: An American classroom

CAST: 15 actors, min. 2 boys (•), 13 girls (+)

+ Melissa, Age 14
+ Andrea, Age 14
• Brian, Age 14
+ Ms. Torrella, Teacher
• Mr. Shaffer, Teacher
+ Jeanne Villepreux-Power
+ Maria Mitchell
+ Ellen Swallow Richards

+ En Hedu Anna
+ Gargi
+ Hypatia
+ Mary Kies
+ Ellen Eglui
+ Lady Augusta Lovelace
+ Madame Curie

STAGE SET: small table and chair at down right; 8' by 8' two-level riser at mid-center and an 8' by 8' one-level riser at mid-left

PROPS: paper, pencil, hand mirror, science book, reference book

MUSIC: *We Are All Gifted*

COSTUMES: Melissa, Andrea, Brian, Ms. Torrella and Mr. Shaffer dress in standard contemporary school attire; En Hedu Anna, Gargi and Hypatia wear women's garb of ancient times — loose-fitting robe or sari (Gargi) with aristocratic headdress or jewelry incorporating astronomical motifs; Mary Kies wears costume of an early 19th-century American farm woman — simple dark long dress, shawl, bonnet; Ellen Eglui wears costume of a late 19th-century American working woman — domestic servant's uniform with an apron or cap; Lady Augusta Lovelace wears costume of an English noblewoman c. 1850 — dark crinoline skirt, lace blouse, velvet jacket, white gloves and jaunty riding hat; Jeanne Villepreux-Power wears French countrywoman's attire of c. 1830 — long flowing skirt, colorful belt sash, loose-fitting blouse and a wide-brimmed straw hat; Maria Mitchell wears costume of 1840's

American city woman — similar to Lady Lovelace but less colorful and less elegant with no hat; Ellen Swallow Richards wears costume of an 1880s' female college professor — long dark formal dress or white blouse and long skirt, hair pulled back tightly; Madame Curie wears a modern white lab uniform and lab coat and perhaps a mouth mask or other chemical lab accessories

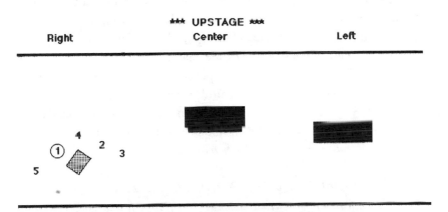

Stage Plan — *Mothers and Daughters of Invention: 4,000 Years of Women in Science*

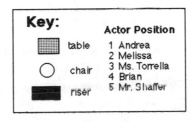

LIGHTS UP RIGHT on twin sisters ANDREA and MELISSA at down right. Andrea sits at a table doing science homework and writing in a notebook; Melissa primps in a hand mirror, fussing with her hair.

MELISSA: Andrea, do you think my hair looks better like this? Or this? This? Or this?

(Andrea continues to write.)

MELISSA: Andrea! I need your help! I'm meeting Brian in a few minutes, and I have to know which way he'll like my hair!

ANDREA: *(Looks up, distracted.)* I'm sorry, Melissa. What did you say?

MELISSA: My sister, lost in the ozone again!

ANDREA: Close. I'm finishing up a report on solar radiation, and ozone does absorb the sun's most harmful ultraviolet rays.

MELISSA: Science wonk! I do *not* understand why you waste your time with all that techy mumbo-jumbo! Girls don't need to know science! *(Continues to fool with her hair.)*

(LIGHTS FADE UP CENTER AND LEFT as a teacher, MS. TORRELLA, carrying a reference book, enters from left and crosses slowly to down right.)

ANDREA: But I like science, Melissa. It tells you neat stuff about how things work.

MELISSA: Like what?

ANDREA: Like how hair grows. And what it's made of. And what kind of shampoo cleans your hair best. And, oh, what about pheromones? Those are the chemical substances we have inside us that attract people to one another.

MELISSA: Really? Well, *that's* useful. But it's just all a modern fad. Women never had to mess with science before.

MS. TORRELLA: Actually, they've been "messing" with science for about four thousand years.

MELISSA: *(Whirls around, surprised.)* Oh, Ms. Torrella! I'm sorry!

MS. TORRELLA: That's all right, Melissa. You're still in middle school. It's okay to not know everything about the world. But you should know something about the heritage of women in science. *(Opens reference book.)*

(EN HEDU ANNA enters from left and stands at down center facing audience.)

MS. TORRELLA: The very first woman's name linked with science is En Hedu Anna, who lived in Babylonia during the Third Millennium before Christ.

EN HEDU ANNA: I am chief priestess of the Moon Goddess and daughter of Sargon, ruler of Akkad. My position is one of great power and prestige. Without my favor, no leader can achieve a legitimate claim to rule. My priests and priestesses watch the movement of the stars and direct every activity of trade, farming and crafts. I am the caretaker of my people.

(GARGI enters from left and stands next to En Hedu Anna at down center facing audience.)

GARGI: I am Gargi, a natural philosopher of ancient India. My name is found in the great books of Sanskrit literature — the Vedas — where I am honored as one of the great natural philosophers. Likewise, in Greece, there were many women of learning. Aglaonike was the first astronomer to predict solar and lunar eclipses. Diotama was the teacher of the great philosopher Socrates. And the philosopher Theano was the wife of the brilliant mathematician Pythagoras. After his death, she conducted his school and wrote some of the early works on algebra.

(HYPATIA enters from left and stands next to Gargi at down center facing audience.)

HYPATIA: I am Hypatia of Alexandria, Egypt. I lived during the fourth century A.D. and taught mathematics and natural philosophy at the Library of Alexandria, the greatest library in the world. Scholars from around the world came to visit me and read my treatises on geometry and algebra. But we are living in dangerous times. Many people are frightened of knowledge and of those who challenge their views on the world. To teach superstitions as truth is a most terrible thing. Reserve your right to think, for even to think wrongly is better than not to think at all.

(En Hedu Anna, Gargi and Hypatia cross to riser at mid-center, where they stand at top level and face audience; BRIAN enters from right but is not seen by other characters.)

ANDREA: Wow, Hypatia sounds like a really major scholar!

MS. TORRELLA: She was. But her influence was deeply resented by certain politicians. They incited a mob that killed her and burned the Alexandria Library to the ground.

MELISSA: Well, all that stargazing about philosophy sounds like an awesome slumber party, but did they ever do anything practical? *(Sees Brian.)* Brian!

BRIAN: *(Steps into classroom.)* Hi, everybody! You know, Ms. Torrella, I was on the internet the other night and read about some women that invented practical things in ancient times. Shi Dun was an empress of China who developed the first paper. Nor Mahal of India made the first cashmere shawls and perfume. She was the aunt of the guy the Taj Mahal was built for. Mary Hebraea lived in Egypt and discovered the formula for hydrochloric acid. And Hypatia, didn't she invent a bunch of tools? Like an instrument for distilling water and one for measuring the specific gravity of water? And the astrolabe and the planisphere? Hi, Andrea.

ANDREA: Hi, Brian.

(Melissa grimaces and silently mimics Andrea's "Hi, Brian!")

MELISSA: Gee whiz, Brian, I didn't know you were so, like, into science.

BRIAN: Sure. Isn't everybody?

ANDREA: What about women in medieval times? Were they allowed to do things, or were they just made to be house-serfs?

MS. TORRELLA: Well, society in general wasn't too free at that time for women *or* men — particularly in Europe where the feudal system was still in place. But some women were able to make an impact on the realm of knowledge. There were physicians such as Dorotea Bucca and naturalists like Maria Sibylla Merian and Tarquinia Molza...the mathematicians Maria Agnesi and Sophia Germain, the physicists Maria Angela Ardinghelli and Emilie de Breteuil and the astronomers Caroline Herschel, Marie Cunitz, Maria Kirch and the 16th-century Danish astronomer Sophia Brahe, whose observations helped her brother Tycho Brahe make his revolutionary discoveries about our planets. There were also noted composers including Hildegard, the Abbess of St. Rupert in Germany, who developed the music of Gregorian chant, and Sister Juana Inez de la Cruz, a nun who lived in Mexico City in the 1600s and also painted and observed the stars. When she was asked if studying science would interfere with her religious faith, Sister Juana replied, "Science and knowledge will strengthen faith in God, not weaken it." And it was in the New World of the Americas that women's ingenuity came to find fuller expression.

(MARY KIES and ELLEN EGLUI enter from left and stand at down center facing audience.)

MARY KIES: My name is Mary Kies, an American inventor. On May 5, 1809, I received the first United States patent granted to a woman. It was for a new, inexpensive method of weaving straw with silk. This was quite important, since at the time most women worked in the fields and wore bonnets to shield themselves from the weather.

ELLEN EGLUI: I am Ellen Eglui from Washington, D.C., and I've worked hard all my life. I invented the clothes wringer for washing machines so other women won't have to work as hard getting their clothes clean. But I had to sell that patent in 1888 for eighteen dollars, because you know I am black, and if it was known that a Negro woman patented the invention, white ladies would not buy the wringer — or so I was told by my attorney.

MARY KIES: Ellen was not the only woman not getting full credit for her ideas. Catherine Green lived in the late 1700s and made key contributions to the invention of a working cotton gin that *Mr.* Eli Whitney later patented.

ELLEN EGLUI: And Sybilla Masters around the same time in colonial Philadelphia. Her husband received a British patent for an invention *she* created — a new method of curing Indian corn that helped feed millions of people.

MARY KIES: Mary Brush received a U.S. patent for a corset in 1825.

ELLEN EGLUI: Sarah Mather received a patent in 1845 for the submarine telescope and lamp.

MARY KIES: Eliza Luca Pinckney developed techniques for indigo cultivation.

ELLEN EGLUI: And one of the most practical inventions of all time — the computer — was guided to life by a woman, Lady Augusta Lovelace of England, who lived from 1815 to 1851.

(LADY AUGUSTA LOVELACE enters from left and stands next to Ellen Eglui at down center facing audience.)

LADY AUGUSTA LOVELACE: I guess you might say I was the first computer programmer. I am the daughter of Lord Byron, the poet, and spent my short life using our family fortune to support artists and inventors of both sexes. One of my patrons was Sir Charles Babbage, the inventor of the first mechanical computer he called an "analytical engine." Of course, there was a small problem. Charles had built this delightful machine with all sorts of levers and pulleys and wheels and gears, but it just sat there. It didn't know what to do with itself! So I wrote the "code" to run the machine, which Charles put onto little paper cards that gave the machine commands. And it just purred right along!

(Mary Kies, Ellen Eglui and Lady Augusta Lovelace cross to riser at

*mid-center, where they stand on first level and face audience; MR.
SHAFFER enters from right.)*

ANDREA: Hi, Mr. Shaffer!

MR. SHAFFER: Just walking down the hall when I heard this fascinating discussion. Did you know that between 1895 and 1910, over
three thousand women received patents from the U.S. government?
At the end of the 19th century, science really came into its own,
and women played a major role.

*(JEANNE VILLEPREUX-POWER, MARIA MITCHELL and
ELLEN SWALLOW RICHARDS enter from left and stand at down
center facing audience.)*

JEANNE VILLEPREUX-POWER: Je m'appelle Jeanne Villepreux-
Power of France, a shoemaker's daughter born in 1794. As a child
I was taught the womanly art of sewing, which stood me in good
stead throughout my life. I left my small village and walked to Paris,
where I became a dressmaker's assistant and created a wedding gown
for a princess. A rich Englishman saw the dress and married me.
Can you believe it? Just like Cinderella, oui? Well, we moved to
Sicily, where we lived on the beautiful Mediterranean Sea. I became
fascinated by the sea and taught myself about the natural sciences.
In 1832 I created the first aquarium for scientific research. By the
time I died in 1871, I had written several books on marine envi-
ronments and was known as "the mother of aquatic science."

MARIA MITCHELL: I am Maria Mitchell of Nantucket Island,
Massachusetts. When I grew up in the 1820s, I was not permitted
to attend formal school, being "only a girl." But I studied with my
father at home and learned from books at the library…and in 1847
I discovered a comet! The following year I was the first woman
appointed to the Academy of Arts and Sciences. Throughout the
century I continued to teach astronomy at universities and make
several important contributions to the field. I built an observatory
next to my home on Nantucket Island, the Maria Mitchell
Observatory. You can visit it today, if you like.

ELLEN SWALLOW RICHARDS: My name is Ellen Swallow Richards, engineer. In the 1870s I founded the science of home economics, which simplifies and systematizes housework and shows how to provide nutritious meals at reasonable cost. I was the first woman to enter a technical institute, the Massachusetts Institute of Technology, where I studied chemistry. After graduating, I continued to work at the Institute testing commercial products and doing quality tests on air, water and soil, for which I have been called the founder of ecology. But the greatest woman scientist of the day was our renowned colleague from France, the two-time winner of the Nobel Prize for scientific accomplishment, Madame Curie.

(MADAME CURIE enters from left and stands at down left as Ellen Swallow Richards, Maria Mitchell, Jeanne Villepreux-Power and the other historic women on the riser applaud.)

MADAME CURIE: Merci beaucoups, mes amis. I was born in Poland in 1867. Together with my husband, Pierre, also a chemist, we pioneered the earliest research on radioactivity. In 1898 we discovered the atomic elements radium and polonium and, after Pierre died, I succeeded in isolating pure radium.

JEANNE VILLEPREUX-POWER: You are too modest, madame. These experiments created the field of nuclear chemistry and changed forever the course of science.

MADAME CURIE: One never notices what has been done; one can only see what remains to be done.

MARIA MITCHELL: Madame Curie gave her life for science. She died in 1934 from leukemia caused by her experiments with radiation.

MADAME CURIE: Life is not easy for any of us. But what of that? We must have perseverance and, above all, confidence in ourselves. We must believe that we are gifted for something, and that this thing — at whatever cost — must be attained. Nothing in life is to be feared. It is only to be understood.

(Jeanne Villepreux-Power, Maria Mitchell, Ellen Swallow Richards and

Madame Curie cross to riser at mid-left, where they stand and face audience.)

ANDREA: These women really had a hunger for science.

MS. TORRELLA: And so do women today. In the last fifteen years American women have earned over fifteen thousand Ph.D.s in scientific fields. And students in medicine and dentistry are at least fifty per cent female.

ANDREA: And women are still inventing things. My parents were talking about a woman named Stephanie Kwolek who invented the product called Kevlar that police use for bullet-proof vests.

MELISSA: Who? When did they talk about something like that?

ANDREA: Usually every night after supper — when you have your nose buried in television!

MR. SHAFFER: Stephanie Kwolek was a chemist for Du Pont and also discovered patents related to fiber-optic cables, aircraft parts, canoes, film and hundreds of polymer-based products.

MS. TORRELLA: Maria Telkes designed the first solar house in the 1930s. Katherine Blodgett invented nonreflecting glass.

MR. SHAFFER: Rosalind Franklin discovered the helix shape of DNA in the 1950s. Elizabeth Lee Hazen and Rachel Fuller Brown discovered the world's first antifungal antibiotic.

MS. TORRELLA: Evelyn Boyd Granville made important contributions to the U.S. space program. Barbara McClintock won the Nobel Prize in 1983 for discoveries in genetics.

MR. SHAFFER: Patsy Sherman patented Scotchguard Tape, Bette Nesmith Graham invented Liquid Paper and Patricia Billings of Kansas City, Missouri, discovered Geobond — a building material that is indestructible and fireproof, one of the most revolutionary substances in the history of construction.

BRIAN: Didn't the Hollywood actress Hedy Lamarr invent a secret military code that helped the United States win World War II?

ANDREA: I read that the cosmetics inventor Madame C.J. Walker was the first woman millionaire ever!

MS. TORRELLA: And don't forget the mathematician and Navy officer Grace Hopper, who just died in 1992. She was the driving force behind modern computer technology. *(Looks at watch.)* Study hall's almost over. Good talking to you. *(Exits right.)*

MR. SHAFFER: So long, everybody. *(Exits right.)*

ANDREA: *(To Melissa.)* So, you see, sister — women in science isn't just a fad.

MELISSA: I stand corrected. And speaking of standing…Brian, did you have something you wanted to ask me?

BRIAN: Huh? No. I just dropped by to see if Andrea would like to get a milk shake after school.

ANDREA: I'd love to, Brian.

BRIAN: Great. Would you want to go to the library afterwards? We've got that big science test coming up, and I always study better with someone really smart.

ANDREA: No problem. Will you walk me to class?

BRIAN: Sure. So long, Melissa.

(Andrea and Brian exit right; Melissa scowls, folds her arms, impatiently taps her feet and then studies herself in her hand mirror.)

MELISSA: Hmmm. Maybe I *could* be an astronomer like that Maria Mitchell. I wonder what I'd look like in one of those astronaut helmet doodads? Probably wouldn't mess up my hair *too* much. And I could really get into shopping on Venus! *(Exits right.)*

EN HEDU ANNA: The wonders of science have no gender. Men and women alike are partners in the discovery of our universe.

MARY KIES: As the 20th-century astronomer Cecilia Payne-Gaposchkin said—

ELLEN EGLUI: The reward of the young scientist is the emotional thrill of being the first person in the history of the world to see something or to understand something. Nothing can compare with that experience.

MARIA MITCHELL: To those who have said women are not suited to science, I say this: The eye that directs the needle in the delicate meshes of embroidery will equally well bisect a star with the spider web of the micrometer.

(ALL HISTORIC CHARACTERS sing. Music: "We Are All Gifted.")

ALL HISTORIC CHARACTERS: *(Sing.)*
> We are all gifted, each and every one
> Eager to seek out our place in the sun.
> Searching and striving for knowledge and truth,
> Our quest is unending, horizons unbound
> As we set our course toward the stars spinning round.
> We are all gifted; let our flag of hope and faith unfurl
> Brothers and sisters changing the world.

(LIGHTS OUT.)

THE END

We Arc All Gifted

(words & music by L.E. McCullough)

We Are All Gifted, page 2

we set our course toward the stars spinn- ing round.

We are all gift- ed; let our flag of

hope and faith un- furl. Bro- thers and sis- ters

chang- ing the we can make a pa- ra- dise ap- pear be- fore our

ve- ry ey- es world.

© L.E. McCullough 1999

Counting, from Quipu to Googol

We usually think of mathematics as a very exact science. But it wasn't always so, because until just a few hundred years ago, people couldn't agree on what numbers were or how they should be written. Many different systems of numbers existed throughout the world in ancient times. Often numbers were associated with events in nature such as the movement of the stars and planets or even elements of religious and civic ritual. Tools used for counting and calculating were also very simple — sticks, pieces of rope, counting boards and the abacus...often simply fingers and toes! Still, much of the mathematical knowledge we enjoy today was made possible by the inspiration of brilliant scientists and inventors: the Frenchman Blaise Pascal invented a primitive mechanical calculator in 1642; in 1835 Charles Babbage of England designed an "analytical engine" — the forerunner of the modern computer.

RUNNING TIME: 20 minutes

TIME: Yesterday morning

PLACE: Just a block or two from school

CAST: 12 actors, min. 3 boys (•), 2 girls (+)
+ Beth, age 10 or so
+ Mika, age 10 or so
North American Indian
Sumerian
• Aryabhata
• Al-Khwarizmi

• Zed (speaks in an English accent)
Neolithic Human
2 Incas
Egyptian
Roman

STAGE SET: mid-sized box or cube at down left (strong enough for sitting on, large enough to conceal an abacus and counting board)

PROPS: math book, 8 pebbles, tally stick, sharp-edged stone, illustrated animal skin, 3 quipus, clay tablet and stylus, papyrus, stone tablet, black magic marker, counting board, abacus, parchment, Al-Khwarizmi's book

EFFECTS: Sound — school bell or buzzer

COSTUMES: Beth and Mika wear contemporary school clothes; Zed wears a porkpie hat with mathematical symbols and equations, a white dress shirt with a big zero painted on it, a colorful bow tie, floppy shoes or boots; Neolithic Human wears cave dweller dress (animal skins); North American Indian wears traditional Native American garb — moccasins, buckskin breeches and shirt; Incas wear peasant attire of medieval Peru; Sumerian, Egyptian and Roman wear period costume of ancient Middle East and Mediterranean; Aryabhata wears a long plain-colored robe; Al-Khwarizmi wears a long plain-colored robe with a brightly-colored belt-sash and a turban

PRONUNCIATION: *Neolithic* — Nee-o-**lith**-ik
quipu — **kee**-pu
Sumeria — Soo-**mer**-ee-a
stylus — **sty**-lis
hieratic — hy-**ra**-tik
papyrus — pa-**py**-rus
Aryabhata — Ar-ya-**ba**-ta
Al-Khwarizmi — Al-Kwa-**riz** mee

Illustrated Animal Skin

Quipu

Sumerian Clay Tablet

Egyptian Papyrus

Roman Stone Tablet

|	1
	2
	3
ε	4
	5
	6
V	7
٨	8
9	9
•	0

Al-Khwarizmi's Book

LIGHTS UP RIGHT AND CENTER on BETH entering from right holding a math book in her arms as she makes her way slowly toward center, muttering math formulas and fumbling in the pages of her book.

BETH: Okay, fractions. X over Y equals, equals what, equals something, equals Y under X? *(Slams book shut in frustration.)* Ouch!

(MIKA enters from right and walks briskly up to Beth.)

MIKA: Beth, hurry up! You'll be late for school!

BETH: I'm studying, Mika, studying is happening here! Very major studying!

MIKA: Why do you wait till one hour before the big math test to start studying?

BETH: Because I *hate* math, Mika! I despise math! I detest math! I revile, abhor, loathe and utterly scorn math! Did I say I don't even like it much?

MIKA: But math is fun! So many exciting things you can do with formulas and equations!

BETH: Mika, you think watching paint dry is exciting.

MIKA: Math is like an entire universe — an entire universe built on numbers!

(SOUND: school bell or buzzer.)

MIKA: Oops, there's the first bell! We've got five minutes to class! *(Skips offstage left.)*

(Beth continues to mutter and walk in a circle at down center, engrossed in her math book, not paying attention to where she's walking.)

BETH: Numbers! I wish there weren't any such thing as numbers. Who needs numbers, anyway? *(Looks up.)* Hey, where am I? This isn't Pebble Lane!

(LIGHTS UP LEFT on ZED sitting at down left on a box, toying with a handful of pebbles.)

ZED: It certainly is. Only we're going to call it Calculus Street for awhile.

BETH: Excuse me?

ZED: Of course you know the word "calculus" is the Latin word for "pebble." And pebbles were used in ancient Rome as a device for counting.

BETH: I think this is the part where I yell for the police. But before the funny farm people take you away, what is your name, most unusually-dressed, silly-talking crazy person?

ZED: *(Stands and offers handshake, from which Beth recoils.)* Sorry, we haven't been properly introduced. I'm Zed. Spelled Z-E-D. That's what we British call the letter Z, which stands for "zero," which is what your life would be without numbers. *(Raises arms and hands together, then flings them apart.)* Numbers, begone! *(Points skyward as if watching a flock of birds.)* There they go! All the numbers in the world are gone. You're safe now!

BETH: *(Rubs her eyes.)* Pancakes and sushi for breakfast was not a good idea! *(Shivers.)* Brrr! It's cold! I should have worn a jacket today!

ZED: But how could you have known how cold it would be? You don't have any numbers to tell you. I hear it's your birthday next week.

BETH: You bet! And I'm having a big party!

ZED: I'd like to buy you a present. When is the party?

BETH: It's — ummm, let's see…it's, uh—

ZED: You don't know the date, so I guess no one will come to your party. How old will you be?

BETH: I'll be, let's see…ummm…*(Holds her hands in front of her, then sticks out both palms.)* This many?

ZED: I could still get you a present. How about some new sneakers? Great for soccer!

BETH: Yeh!

ZED: What size shoe do you wear?

BETH: Size? Ummm, gosh…kinda large, but not *too* large…maybe "average?"

ZED: The school basketball team played last night.

BETH: Who won?

ZED: The team that had the highest score.

BETH: Score? What's a score?

ZED: Maybe you'd like to go see the Spice Street Boys in concert next week?

BETH: Yeh!

ZED: How much are tickets?

BETH: Ummm...*(Scratches head.)*

ZED: Your family is taking a trip to the park this weekend. How far is it?

BETH: Ummm...

ZED: When is your Aunt Sally coming to town?

BETH: Ummm...

ZED: You're going to meet her at the airport. At which gate will her plane be?

BETH: Ummm...look, all these questions—

ZED: What's your address?

BETH: I don't know.

ZED: What's your phone number?

BETH: I don't know.

ZED: What's your mom's pager ID?

BETH: *(Growing more agitated.)* I don't know!

ZED: What's your locker number?

BETH: I don't know!

ZED: That book looks heavy. How much does it weigh?

BETH: I don't know!

ZED: My goodness, you look absolutely feverish! How fast is your heart beating?

BETH: I'm telling you, I *don't know!*

ZED: Of course you don't! Because there aren't any numbers in your life!

BETH: Oh, right. Then how do people count things?

ZED: I was hoping you'd ask. *(Joins Beth at down center.)*

(NEOLITHIC HUMAN enters from right holding a tally stick and a sharp-edged stone and stands at down right.)

ZED: If we were living in very ancient times, say the Neolithic Period —
or Stone Age, as it's commonly called — we would use a tool called
a "tally stick" to keep count of things.

NEOLITHIC HUMAN: Every day I go hunting, I take this sharp stone
and carve a notch in this stick. *(Exits right.)*

ZED: The tally stick system was used for centuries by rural people
throughout the world. It was even used in England by tax collec-
tors up until the 1830s.

*(NORTH AMERICAN INDIAN enters from left holding an illustrated
animal skin and stands at down left.)*

ZED: The native peoples of North America used tally sticks but also
drew symbols to show quantities.

NORTH AMERICAN INDIAN: *(Displays animal skin to Zed and
Beth.)* I have five buffalo skins. You have a bow and eight arrows.
I would like to trade my five skins for your bow and eight arrows.
Deal? *(Exits left.)*

ZED: A more sophisticated method of tally keeping was by tying knots
onto a length of rope or cord. This system was used in ancient
Greece, China, Africa and Polynesia. But nowhere was it used with
such intricacy as among the Inca people of South America.

*(TWO INCA enter from right, each carrying a quipu, and stand at
down right.)*

INCA #1: *(Displays quipu to Zed and Beth.)* This is called a "quipu,"
which is the Inca word for "knot." Each knot on the quipu stands
for a single unit. Here, I have a quipu that tells me the number of
sheep in my herd.

INCA #2: *(Displays two quipus to Zed and Beth.)* I have both sheep and
goats in my herd. This quipu is a blue cord and represents the
number of sheep. The other quipu is red and represents the number
of goats. As you can tell by looking, I have four sheep and seven
goats.

INCA #1: I have fifty sheep. On my quipu, each knot stands for ten sheep. If I had fifty-one sheep, I would tie a smaller knot — or a knot with a double twist — to represent the different single unit.

(Incas exit right.)

BETH: Zed, I have a question.

ZED: Yes?

BETH: A quipu and tally stick would be okay if you could *show* it. But how could you prove how many animals you had if you didn't carry every one of your sticks and quipus around all the time?

ZED: Precisely. What you need is a way of showing the amounts independently of the tool you use to count them. Enter the "numeral!"

(SUMERIAN enters from left carrying a clay tablet and stylus and stands at down left.)

ZED: About six thousand years ago, just northwest of the Persian Gulf, was an empire called Sumeria. The Sumerians were the first people to build cities. They were also the first people to develop a writing system using a special tool called a "stylus" — a cylinder shaped like a pencil — that made marks when pressed into clay tablets.

SUMERIAN: Our writing system was based on syllables, and it used signs to indicate different numerals. *(Displays tablet to Zed and Beth.)* We Sumerians also invented fractions and the numeric place system, whereby the position of each numeral in the number tells you its value. *(Exits left.)*

BETH: How come I've never heard of Sumeria?

ZED: Sumeria was conquered by the Babylonian Empire in the 20th century B.C. The Babylonians took their numeral system and passed it on to the Egyptians.

(EGYPTIAN enters from right carrying a papyrus and stands at down right.)

EGYPTIAN: We advanced the Sumerian concept of numerals and added more signs. See? *(Displays papyrus to Zed and Beth.)* Here are numerals for one, ten, one hundred, one thousand, ten thousand, one hundred thousand and one million.

BETH: Each numeral is a picture!

(Beth puts her math book on ground at down center and crosses to examine papyrus.)

ZED: That's the "hieratic" style of writing, which the Egyptians used on sheets of parchment called "papyrus."

EGYPTIAN: One is a papyrus leaf.

BETH: Ten is a papyrus leaf tied and bent.

ZED: One hundred is a piece of rope.

EGYPTIAN: One thousand is a lotus flower

BETH: Ten thousand is a snake.

ZED: One hundred thousand is a tadpole.

EGYPTIAN: And a million is a scribe with his arms raised to the boundless, everlasting heavens. *(Exits right.)*

BETH: That seems really simple!

ZED: It is. But as time passed, the world grew larger and more complex. By the time the Roman Empire came into its full glory, there were many more things to count.

(ROMAN enters from left carrying a stone tablet and stands at down left.)

ROMAN: Roman numerals are a supremely logical system. You have seven basic signs that are also letters in the alphabet.

BETH: I know them! An I stands for one, a V stands for five and X stands for ten.

ZED: L stands for fifty.

BETH: C stands for one hundred.

ZED: D stands for five hundred.

BETH: And M stands for one thousand.

ROMAN: Correct. *(Displays tablet to Zed and Beth.)* Do you know what this number is?

BETH: Hmmm…an X means ten, the C means one hundred, the I means one and the last X means ten. One hundred twenty-one?

ROMAN: Incorrect. Centurion! Take this ignoramus to the lion pit!

ZED: Hold on a moment. You see, the Romans were clever and figured out ways to use as few letters as possible. *(Takes black magic marker from pants pocket and writes on back of Roman's stone tablet.)* Instead of writing the number nine as V and then four Is, they put the I in front of the sign for ten — the X — which made IX a nine.

ROMAN: And an X in front of a C would indicate the number ninety.

BETH: I get it. So, the X is being subtracted from the C, not the C added to the X.

ROMAN: Correct.

BETH: Which is ten from a hundred — or ninety.

ROMAN: Correct again.

BETH: And the I and X aren't eleven, they're nine.

ROMAN: Correct once more.

BETH: So this number is ninety-nine!

ROMAN: Correct yet again. But I still say she belongs in the lion pit. *(Exits left.)*

BETH: Roman numerals can be confusing if you don't know where the numeral starts.

ZED: Right you are. And the other problem is that Roman numerals don't allow for addition and subtraction, or any kind of mathematical function among numbers. They just sort of lie there on the tablet. So the Romans came up with a "counting board."

(Zed reaches behind box, takes out a counting board and sets it on the box, then pulls several pebbles from his pocket and tosses them on the board.)

ZED: The board is divided into three columns — column one for ones, column two for tens, column three for hundreds. And each pebble—

BETH: A calculus!

ZED: Stands for one unit. When you get ten pebbles in the ones column, you replace them with one pebble in the tens column.

BETH: I guess that makes sense. But with only three columns, you can't have very large numbers.

ZED: That problem was solved by a device called the "abacus."

(Zed puts counting board behind box, takes out an abacus and displays it to Beth.)

BETH: I know what that is! It's a counting thingamajigie from China!

ZED: Well, let's be a bit more precise, shall we? The abacus was first used in ancient Greece and Rome and didn't come into general favor in China until about the twelfth century A.D. But the Chinese became absolute masters at the abacus, and it is still very popular there today.

BETH: It's a wooden frame divided in two parts by a bar in the middle. And it has nine little rods that go from the top to bottom of the frame.

ZED: And each rod has seven beads — two in the top section, five in the bottom. Numbers are counted and calculated by moving beads up to the middle bar.

BETH: That's really cool! But it still seems like a lot of work to figure things out on it.

ZED: That's because the abacus, like the counting board, is still dependent upon physical objects to represent abstract numbers. But all that changed around 500 A.D., after the Roman Empire had fallen and the light of scientific inquiry began to shine brightly in the East.

(ARYABHATA enters from right carrying a parchment and stands at down right.)

ARYABHATA: I am the astronomer Aryabhata, from India. In our system, the value of a numeral depends upon its place in the number. *(Displays parchment to Zed and Beth.)* This number for example, means that there are four hundreds, three tens and no ones.

BETH: Four hundred thirty!

ARYABHATA: You are a brilliant child. Do you notice anything unusual about this number?

BETH: Hmmm. It has a zero!

ARYABHATA: Your mind is a flowering lotus. The zero was discovered by the Maya people of Central America around six hundred years before the birth of your Jesus Christ. Here in India, we began using zero about 200 B.C., and we have found it very useful. *(exits right)*

ZED: Oh, but not half as useful as the learned elders of the Arabic Empire, which conquered India around 700 A.D. One of them, Al-Khwarizmi, lived in Baghdad and wrote the first book that explained decimals. It was called "The Book on Addition and Subtraction by Indian Methods."

(AL-KHWARIZMI enters from left carrying a book and stands at down left.)

AL-KHWARIZMI: We Arabic scholars were the first to work with numbers on their own. Throw away your tally sticks and counting boards! *(Opens book and displays it to Zed and Beth.)*

BETH: Those numbers are a lot like the numbers we have today!

ZED: They *are* the numbers we have today. The symbols on the left show how the numbers were written by Arabs in the Eastern part of the Islamic Empire. The symbols on the right were from the West and later became our numbers.

AL-KHWARIZMI: These ten numerals — including the most sublime zero — will stand for any number in the universe, no matter how big!

ZED: Even a googol?

AL-KHWARIZMI: Yes, even a googol! Whatever that may be! *(Exits left.)*

BETH: What *is* a googol?

ZED: Pretty much the highest known number in the universe. The googol is the numeral 1 followed by 100 zeros. Edward Kasner, an American mathematician, coined it in 1938 from listening to the baby talk of his little nephew, Milton.

BETH: Having a number named after you! That's awesome!

ZED: Numbers are awesome. They shape and transform everything we know about the universe. Numbers make engines and airplanes possible, computers and skyscrapers, heart pumps and food processors, machines of every size and description, even a rocket to send men to the moon — and beyond! It's all numbers. It's all math.

BETH: Ohmygosh! My math test! I'm late! Where's my math book!

(Beth looks frantically for her math book; as she searches, Zed circles around her and slips offstage right; LIGHTS FADE OUT RIGHT; offstage left, Mika shouts.)

MIKA: *(O.S.)* Beth! Beth, hurry up!
BETH: *(Finds math book, picks it up.)* Here we go!

(Mika enters from left.)

MIKA: Beth! The second bell is going to ring any minute!
BETH: Any minute? It should have rung hours ago! *(Peers around.)* Where's Zed? And Al-Khwarizmi?
MIKA: Al who?
BETH: Nevermind. Mika, what street is this?
MIKA: Physically, you're on Pebble Lane. But mentally, I think you're a few light years west of Jupiter. Come on! *(Dashes offstage left.)*
BETH: Okay. *(Crosses left to exit, stops, turns to look around stage.)* Numbers — they're not so scary. I'm going to score a googol on that math test!

(LIGHTS OUT. SOUND: school bell or buzzer.)

THE END

"Constellations Then Arise":
Astronomy in the Age of Copernicus

Until the 1500s, most people — educated and uneducated alike — believed the universe was organized on a *geocentric* model, with the Earth as the center of the universe. In 1543, a book called *De revolutionibus orbium coelestium* ("Concerning the Revolution of the Heavenly Spheres") was published by an unknown Polish astronomer and church canon named Nicholaus Copernicus (1473–1543). This book put forth the first convincing proof that the universe followed a *heliocentric* system, in which the Earth and planets in our solar system revolve around the Sun. While Copernicus did not have a complete explanation for all celestial phenomena, future astronomers such as Brahe, Galileo, Kepler, Hooke, Newton, Halley, Herschel and others would use his work as a foundation for great advances in our understanding of how the universe operates.

RUNNING TIME: 20 minutes

TIME: 1574; 1539

PLACE: The town of Frauenberg, Poland

CAST: 11 actors, min. 4 boys (•), 1 girl (+)
- Nicholaus Copernicus, age 66–70   • George Rheticus, age 60
- Philip Melanchthon   • George Rheticus, age 25–29
+ Anna   5 Actors
  Narrator (offstage)

STAGE SET: small writing table and high stool at down right; at down
center a low stool and large table with large globe and pieces of parchment; toward end of play a cot is placed at down left

PROPS: quill pen, pieces of parchment, large globe, plate of bread and
cheese, bread knife, 5–6 coins, old hardbound book

COSTUMES: Nicholaus Copernicus wears a Renaissance professor's
robe and hat (similar to a modern graduation day cap and gown); George
Rheticus Young and Old wear outfits similar to Copernicus but less distinguished; Philip Melanchthon is attired in a monk's habit; Anna wears
a 16th-century servant's outfit — blouse and skirt, perhaps a kerchief
tied around her head; Actors wear *commedia dell'arte*-style costumes and
makeup that exaggerate their characters — the fake Copernicus has a
robe similar to the real Copernicus but wears a dunce cap decorated with
stars, the Peasant has straw sticking out of his cap, the Cow a pair of
horns attached to head and a tail attached to backside, the Sun wears
sun rays attached to head and body, the Moon has a quarter moon on
head.

LIGHTS UP RIGHT on GEORGE RHETICUS/OLD sitting at table at down right, writing on parchment with a quill pen; he speaks to audience.

GEORGE RHETICUS/OLD: Ah, hello! Come in, come in! I am only studying the latest reports of celestial discovery. What a miraculous age we live in! *(Holds up parchment.)* In Denmark, the astronomer Tycho Brahe has sighted a "supernova" — an explosion of stars that scatter an immense shower of light through the universe. Some say such an event heralds the Second Coming! But, why would the Messiah want to return to Earth now, in the year 1574? With all these wars and persecutions upon the land, we are so far from being in a state of heavenly grace. And every day our knowledge of the universe expands ever more. We have so much more to learn before the world comes to an end! What? *(Chuckles.)* Ah, yes, it did seem for awhile that my former master, Nicholaus Copernicus, *was* preparing to bring the world to an end. And I suppose, in a way, he did.

(LIGHTS UP CENTER AND LEFT as GEORGE RHETICUS/ YOUNG enters from left and crosses to down center, looking around the stage in confusion; NICHOLAUS COPERNICUS sits on low stool at table, mostly hidden by the large globe on table. LIGHTS FADE OUT RIGHT.)

GEORGE RHETICUS/OLD: I came to study with Copernicus in 1539, when he was Canon of the Cathedral of Frauenberg — a humble but demanding post he had held for nearly thirty years. I was a young man of twenty-five, with a degree in mathematics from the University of Wittenberg. Oh, I thought I knew everything about the sciences! But I would soon learn otherwise.

GEORGE RHETICUS/YOUNG: Canon Copernicus? It is George Rheticus, your new assistant!

(Nicholaus Copernicus raises his head from behind globe.)

NICHOLAUS COPERNICUS: You have already given yourself the position without the bother of an interview?

GEORGE RHETICUS/YOUNG: *(Startled.)* I beg your pardon, Canon! I did not realize you were in the room.

NICHOLAUS COPERNICUS: And yet I was here all the time. *(Spins the globe.)* Were that the process of discovery always that simple. What do you know of astronomy?

GEORGE RHETICUS/YOUNG: *(Clears throat.)* Well, there are many theories. The ancient Greeks believed the Earth was a flat island riding on an infinite sea. The Egyptians said the god Ra rode his boat across the sky as upon a river. At night, he rode back, bringing darkness in his wake.

NICHOLAUS COPERNICUS: Yes, yes, but what of the Greek philosopher Thales?

GEORGE RHETICUS/YOUNG: He said the Earth was surrounded by a series of concentric spheres.

NICHOLAUS COPERNICUS: Including?

GEORGE RHETICUS/YOUNG: Including the five planets — Mercury, Venus, Mars, Jupiter, Saturn — and our Earth moon. And the Sun and the stars. His student Anaximander said Earth was surrounded by a hollow sphere of stars.

(ANNA enters from left, carrying a plate of bread and cheese, which she sets on table at down center; she is unnoticed by Copernicus and Rheticus.)

NICHOLAUS COPERNICUS: And?

GEORGE RHETICUS/YOUNG: And these viewpoints were combined by Ptolemy in the second century after Christ to form his theory that the Earth is indeed the center of the universe.

ANNA: Poppycock!

GEORGE RHETICUS/YOUNG: I beg your pardon, madame!

NICHOLAUS COPERNICUS: Anna is my housekeeper.

ANNA: Ptolemy was an imbecile! He made up facts to fit his fancy!

NICHOLAUS COPERNICUS: She holds very strong opinions on certain subjects.

ANNA: Ptolemy completely ignored retrograde motion.

GEORGE RHETICUS/YOUNG: I beg your pardon! He explained it fully!

NICHOLAUS COPERNICUS: Ah, but did he explain it correctly? Retrograde motion, as we know, is the phenomena of planets traveling backward across our sky.

ANNA: When it is clear they should be traveling forward.

NICHOLAUS COPERNICUS: If the Earth were indeed the center of the universe, no planet should travel backward in the sky.

ANNA: And if Mercury and Venus travel around the Earth, they should move *away* from the Sun, which they never do.

GEORGE RHETICUS/YOUNG: I beg your pardon, but what am I to think?

NICHOLAUS COPERNICUS: Just think, my boy, just think! That is the first step.

ANNA: Canon, your mid-day meal. You must take nourishment.

NICHOLAUS COPERNICUS: Thank you, Anna. *(To Rheticus.)* Join me, please.

(Anna exits left; Copernicus goes to table at mid-center and begins cutting bread.)

NICHOLAUS COPERNICUS: Does the name Aristarchus mean anything to you.

GEORGE RHETICUS/YOUNG: Aristarchus of Samos? He lived in the third century before Our Lord.

NICHOLAUS COPERNICUS: And?

GEORGE RHETICUS/YOUNG: He suggested that the Earth revolves around the Sun.

NICHOLAUS COPERNICUS: And?

GEORGE RHETICUS/YOUNG: And, no one believed him.

(Copernicus arranges bread and cheese chunks on plate to form a model of the solar system.)

NICHOLAUS COPERNICUS: But what if it were true? What if the

Sun — our delicious cheese — were the center of the universe? And the planets — Earth included, here, here, here and here — revolved around the Sun along orbits of varying length, like so?

(Copernicus moves a bread chunk around the cheese.)

GEORGE RHETICUS/YOUNG: Then retrograde motion would be an illusion. Other planets would only seem to swim backward across the sky because the Earth overtakes them on its orbit around the Sun.

(Copernicus moves two bread chunks close to the cheese.)

NICHOLAUS COPERNICUS: Therefore Mercury and Venus appear to be close to the Sun, because they are. Say that Mercury orbits a shorter distance. In a single Earth year, it would travel around the Sun several times.

GEORGE RHETICUS/YOUNG: And look as if it's moving backwards in relation to Earth.

NICHOLAUS COPERNICUS: Precisely.

GEORGE RHETICUS/YOUNG: *(Takes a bread chunk and eats it.)* This is an interesting theory, Canon Copernicus. Of course, you have no proof of this, other than bread and cheese.

NICHOLAUS COPERNICUS: Ah, but of course, I do.

(Copernicus shows a parchment to Rheticus.)

GEORGE RHETICUS/YOUNG: These tables of planetary motion are astonishing!

NICHOLAUS COPERNICUS: They are obvious, my son. They are written in the sky each night. Anyone on Earth can see them — if they bother to look up.

GEORGE RHETICUS/YOUNG: You must publish this information!

NICHOLAUS COPERNICUS: Impossible!

GEORGE RHETICUS/YOUNG: But it is of vital importance! Mathematicians these days are so unsure of the movements of the

Sun and Moon, they cannot explain or even observe the length of a season. Farmers can no longer rely on the calendar for planting and harvesting crops. These tables will restore harmony and balance.

NICHOLAUS COPERNICUS: *(Shakes head "no.")* Quite the contrary. These tables will cause nothing but trouble—

(SOUND of boisterous shouting and laughter offstage; Anna bursts in from left and runs to down center.)

ANNA: Canon! Come quick!

NICHOLAUS COPERNICUS: What is all the tumult?

ANNA: A troupe of actors in the courtyard. They have gathered a large crowd of vagabonds and ne'er-do-wells!

(FIVE ACTORS enter from left and take up positions at down left, playing to audience. ACTOR #1 is dressed like Copernicus, but wearing a dunce cap decorated with stars on head. ACTOR #2 is dressed like a peasant. ACTOR #3 portrays the Sun and wears sun rays on head and body. ACTOR #4 portrays the Moon and has a quarter moon on head. ACTOR #5 enters on all fours and is dressed like a cow with a pair of horns attached to head and a tail attached to backside. While ACTOR #1 and ACTOR #2 speak opening lines, ACTOR #3 and ACTOR #4 stand behind them silently, hands over their eyes, with ACTOR #5 at side of ACTOR #2. All Actors perform in an exaggerated, burlesque manner.)

ACTOR #2: Master Copernicus! I seek Master Nicholaus Copernicus!

ACTOR #1: I am Nicholaus Copernicus.

ACTOR #2: You? But you do not look like a lunatic!

ACTOR #1: That is because I am an astrologer, oops — astronomer! How may I help you?

ACTOR #2: *(Bows.)* I am but a poor peasant. And this is my cow, Mischka.

ACTOR #5: Mooooo!

ACTOR #2: Mischka is not feeling well. She does not give milk anymore.

ACTOR #5: Mooooo!

ACTOR #1: Maybe she is old? Or all dried up inside?

ACTOR #2: Mischka is confused. She has heard that the Sun no longer spins around the Earth. When it is time for her to give milk in the morning, she thinks it is night and lays down to sleep!

ACTOR #5: Mooooo!

ACTOR #1: Nonsense, my good peasant. The universe is a very simple matter even a cow may understand. For example, we have the Sun.

(ACTOR #3 sashays forward, smiling ludicrously; Actor #2 applauds.)

ACTOR #3: Halllllo!

ACTOR #1: And we have the Moon!

(ACTOR #4 steps forward on tiptoes, peering anxiously; Actor #2 applauds.)

ACTOR #4: Is it dark out? I am afraiiiiiiiiid of the dark!

ACTOR #1: *(To Actor #2.)* And you, sir, are Terra Firma.

ACTOR #2: *(Scratches head in puzzlement.)* But my name is Hans Breitelbücher! Who is this Terra Firma? She sounds like a beauuu-uuuutiful lady!

ACTOR #1: The Earth, you simpleton! Now, in the old days, the Sun and Moon turned around you.

(Actors #3 and #4 begin dancing in a circle around Actor #2.)

ACTORS #3 and #4: *(Humming a silly tune.)* La-la-la! La-la-la!

ACTOR #3: I am the Sun!

ACTOR #4: I am the Moon!

ACTOR #1: But, as of yesterday, everything is changed!

(Actors #3 and #4 stop abruptly; Actor #4 bumps into Actor #3.)

ACTOR #1: In my new universe, the Earth moves around the Sun!

(Actor #3 swats Actor #2.)

ACTOR #3: Get going!

(Actor #3 stands with arms folded, looking regal as Actor #2 plods in a circle around Actor #3.)

ACTOR #3: Faster! And you, Moon! Get in line behind Earth!
ACTOR #4: Yes, O Mighty Sun!

(Actor #4 stumbles behind Actor #2 and both dance and stumble, pushing and shoving in a circle around Actor #3. Rheticus and Anna watch the play with increasing dismay, as Copernicus sits on the stool behind the globe and busies himself with his parchment.)

ACTOR #2: I do not like this new universe, Master Copernicus!
ACTOR #3: Faster!
ACTOR #5: Moooooo!
ACTOR #1: It is a wonderful universe!
ACTOR #3: Faster!
ACTOR #5: Mooooo!
ACTOR #2: Martin Luther will not like this universe!
ACTOR #4: Faster!
ACTOR #1: Perhaps I am wrong. Perhaps the Moon is the center of the universe. Stop! Go backwards!
ACTOR #5: Moooooo!

(Actor #2 begins pushing Actor #4 around the Sun.)

ACTOR #2: That is much better!
ACTOR #3: *(Pouting to Copernicus.)* What about me? *I* want to be the center of the universe!

(Anna seizes bread knife and rushes toward Actors.)

ANNA: Enough! Out! Get out!

(Actors stop play and run offstage left, bowing and begging for money as they exit and avoid Anna. Rheticus tosses a handful of coins at the departing actors. Copernicus continues to ignore the whole uproar.)

ACTOR #1: Very good, madame! Very good! *(Exits.)*

ACTOR #2: Wonderful audience! Thank you! *(Exits.)*

ACTOR #3: Bless you, sir! *(Exits followed by Anna chasing.)*

GEORGE RHETICUS/YOUNG: What impertinent dolts! Canon Copernicus, are you not outraged?

NICHOLAUS COPERNICUS: It no doubt expresses the popular opinion of my work.

GEORGE RHETICUS/YOUNG: And that ridiculous remark about Martin Luther! What does a theologian know of science?

NICHOLAUS COPERNICUS: *(Stands, suddenly concerned.)* Quiet, my son. It is not what theologians know that is dangerous, but what they *think* they know.

(Anna enters from left and stands at down left.)

ANNA: A visitor, Canon Copernicus. He says his name is—

(PHILIP MELANCHTHON enters from left, pushing Anna aside.)

PHILIP MELANCHTHON: Philip Melanchton. Scholar, philosopher—

NICHOLAUS COPERNICUS: And emissary of the noted Martin Luther. Please enter.

(Anna curtsies and exits left; Melanchton strides to down center.)

PHILIP MELANCHTHON: I wish a word with you, Canon.

NICHOLAUS COPERNICUS: I am certain you wish more than one.

PHILIP MELANCHTHON: You have uttered assertions about the nature of the universe. God's universe.

NICHOLAUS COPERNICUS: I have published nothing. And my thoughts belong only to me. And to God.

PHILIP MELANCHTHON: Your thoughts have a much wider audience than you think. They circulate among scholars, as well as the common folk.

GEORGE RHETICUS/YOUNG: That is because they make common sense!

NICHOLAUS COPERNICUS: Please calm yourself. My theory is easily explained. *(Touches globe.)* In the beginning we should remark that the universe is like a globe. Whether because this form is the most perfect of all, or because it is the figure having the greatest volume and so would be especially suitable for comprehending and conserving all things.

PHILIP MELANCHTHON: We have no argument there. Continue.

NICHOLAUS COPERNICUS: You agree the universe is simple in design?

PHILIP MELANCHTHON: Why would God have made it otherwise?

NICHOLAUS COPERNICUS: Then perhaps our human perception of this design is imperfect. I have attempted to restore its simplicity with three basic tenets concerning the heavenly spheres. One, there is no center of all the celestial circles or spheres. Two, the center of the Earth is not the center of the universe but only of gravity and the lunar sphere. Three, all the spheres revolve around the sun as their mid-point and, therefore, the Sun is the center of the universe.

PHILIP MELANCHTHON: Preposterous!

NICHOLAUS COPERNICUS: Upon what grounds?

PHILIP MELANCHTHON: Certain men, either from love or novelty, or to make a display of ingenuity, have concluded that the Earth moves. It is a want of honesty and decency to assert such notions publicly, and the example is pernicious.

NICHOLAUS COPERNICUS: More pernicious to wallow in ignorance.

PHILIP MELANCHTHON: It is the part of a good mind to accept the truth as God revealed it and to acquiesce in it.

NICHOLAUS COPERNICUS: But what if we have mis-read God's revelation?

PHILIP MELANCHTHON: Sacred Scripture tells us that Joshua commanded the sun to stand still and not the Earth.

NICHOLAUS COPERNICUS: Joshua was a prophet not a scientist.

PHILIP MELANCHTHON: You tread dangerously close to heresy.

GEORGE RHETICUS/YOUNG: The Pope himself has approved the Canon's ideas.

PHILIP MELANCHTHON: The Pope! What further evidence is needed of their danger? *(Turns and strides to left exit.)* Why do you go to so much trouble to disprove a system that everyone agrees upon? More so, you have no proof! Copernicus, your name will be reviled by the ages as a charlatan! *(Exits left.)*

NICHOLAUS COPERNICUS: It is indeed wonderful to have the force of your convictions. *(Chuckles.)* Even when they are wrong.

GEORGE RHETICUS/YOUNG: Melanchthon is right in one respect. Until you publish your work, you have no proof.

NICHOLAUS COPERNICUS: The time is not right. I still have questions.

GEORGE RHETICUS/YOUNG: You will always have questions. What worthy scientist does not? But questions lead to answers. And more questions. And more answers.

NICHOLAUS COPERNICUS: You speak with a wisdom beyond your years, my son. But a scientist must be patient. Come, let us go into the observatory.

(LIGHTS OUT LEFT AND CENTER; George Rheticus/Old speaks from darkness at down right.)

GEORGE RHETICUS/OLD: It took me four years to convince the Canon to publish his work. In the meantime, public controversy raged. Finally, on May 24, 1543, it happened—the book *Concerning the Revolution of the Heavenly Spheres* was published, written by Nicholaus Copernicus and dedicated to Pope Paul III. Unfortunately, the author was unable to garner much credit. At the very moment of his greatest achievement, Copernicus lay on his deathbed, paralyzed from a stroke.

(LIGHTS UP LEFT on Nicholaus Copernicus lying on a cot at down left. George Rheticus/Young kneels by his side, showing him a copy of his book.)

GEORGE RHETICUS/YOUNG: With this book, Canon, you have opened the door to a world of knowledge!

NICOLAUS COPERNICUS: *(Weakly.)* No, my son. I have but pushed it slightly ajar. It is now the duty of others to cross the threshhold and walk boldly into the future.

GEORGE RHETICUS/YOUNG: Martin Luther has already given his review. "This fool Copernicus," he says, "wishes to reverse the entire science of astronomy!" Well, what if you have?

NICHOLAUS COPERNICUS: I will be surprised if history remembers the words of either of us. But if the universe is indeed a circle, what does it matter which direction you travel, as long as you follow the path of the stars toward their Creator?

(LIGHTS FADE DOWN LEFT.)

NARRATOR: *(O.S.)* It would take many years before the revolutionary theories of Nicholaus Copernicus were confirmed by astronomers like Tycho Brahe, Johannes Kepler and Galileo Galilei. Then, as now, original ideas that challenged traditional ways of looking at the world were not always welcomed. But the courage to continue exploration in the face of opposition is fundamental to science. As the 17th-century English poet John Donne wrote:

And new philosophy calls all in doubt,
The element of fire is quite put out;
The sun is lost, and the earth, and no man's wit
Can well direct him where to look for it.

And in these constellations then arise
New stars, and old do vanish from our eyes.
We spur, we rein the stars, and in their race
They're diversely content to obey our pace.

(LIGHTS OUT.)

THE END

Around the World with Nellie Bly

Born near Pittsburgh, Pennsylvania, Nellie Bly (1865–1922) was a trail-blazing journalist who wrote about issues not often discussed in news-papers of the day — the impact of social, political and economic policies on working women and children. Her skillful, courageous exposés brought attention to injustices that affected the lives of millions of Americans. But she also had fun! In 1889–90 she journeyed across the globe to see if she could match the fictional record held by a character in Jules Verne's book, *Around the World in Eighty Days*. After making the trip in seventy-two days, Nellie Bly became the most famous woman in the world, and even more people read her exciting newspaper sto-ries. Later, she married and ended up in Austria at the outbreak of World War I. Not permitted to return to America, she resorted to her jour-nalistic talents and became the first woman war correspondent. After the war, she returned to New York and wrote newspaper columns about homeless children before dying of pneumonia in 1922. Nellie's real name, incidentally, was Elizabeth Cochran. Because it was considered unseemly for a woman to write for a newspaper using her own name, she took the *nom de plume* Nelly Bly after the Stephen Foster song *Nelly Bly*. "Nelly" became "Nellie" when a printer accidentally changed the spelling of her byline on an article!

RUNNING TIME: 25 minutes

TIME: 1919; 1876; 1887; 1889

PLACE: An ocean liner crossing the North Atlantic; newspaper office; various travel locations

CAST: 23 actors, min. 8 boys (•), 9 girls (+)

+ Nellie Bly, Age 54   + Pauline Sirker, Age 11
+ Nellie Bly, Age 11   • John Cockerill, *NY World* Editor
+ Nellie Bly, Age 22   • Joseph Pulitzer, *NY World* Publisher
+ Nellie's Mother   • Jules Verne, Author
• Asylum Doctor   + Asylum Warden
+ Asylum Inmate   + Asylum Nurse
+ Newsie   • 2 Egyptian Suitors
  2 Sailors   • Captain of the *Oceanic*
• Health Dept. Doctor   Barbershop Quartet (4 singers)

STAGE SET: 2 ocean liner deck chairs at down left; an office desk and two chairs at mid-center; a riser for Barbershop Quartet at mid-right

PROPS: 2 reporter's notebooks, 2 pencils, hard-cover book, straight stick (2 feet in length), tongue depressor, small thin blanket, water bucket, stuffed monkey, folded notepaper, stethoscope, *New York World* newspapers with these headlines: "Behind Asylum Bars!"; "Nellie in Egypt!"; "Gonged in Hong Kong!"; "Father Time Outdone!"

EFFECTS: Sound — ocean liner horn, baby crying, metal door slamming shut, metal door creaking open, water splashing from bucket onto floor, sea storm/wind noise, lightning crack, crowd cheers

MUSIC: *Nelly Bly* by Stephen Foster

COSTUMES: Nellie Bly, Age 54 wears period dress and raincoat c. 1919, perhaps a simple flowered hat; Nellie Bly, Age 11 wears a simple girl's dress or frock; in newspaper office, Nellie Bly, Age 22 wears late 19th-century women's daily public attire — black or brown dress leather shoes or boots; she wears a plain, ragged dress in the asylum; on her trip she dresses in a plaid ulster raincoat and a small peaked traveling cap; Pauline Sirker wears a plain dress and outdoor coat, plus a beret; Joseph Pulitzer, John Cockerill, Jules Verne and Health Dept. Doctor wear suits and ties; Barbershop Quartet wears matching pin-striped suits with white pants and straw hats; Egyptian Sultors each wear a long white robe and a red fez; Captain of the Oceanic wears sea captain's uniform; Sailors wear dungarees and T-shirts; Newsie wears late 19th-century street urchin clothing; Asylum Nurse and Asylum Doctor wear grey hospital uniforms; Asylum Inmate wears plain dress; Nellie's Mother wears a standard house dress of the 1870s.

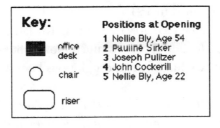

Stage Plan — *Around the World with Nellie Bly*

Around the World with Nellie Bly · 45

STAGE IS DARK. SOUND OFFSTAGE: ocean liner horn sounds twice. LIGHTS UP LEFT on NELLIE BLY, AGE 54 sitting in a deck chair at down left, facing audience, writing in a notebook. A girl, PAULINE SIRKER, enters from right and crosses toward Nellie Bly with a mixture of confidence and hesitation, finally circling around behind Nellie Bly and peeking over her shoulder.

NELLIE BLY, AGE 54: *(Continues to write.)* My dear, even though we are in the middle of a North Atlantic fog thicker than a barrel of Boston bean soup, you are still blocking my light. If you want candy, see the bursar on the foredeck.

PAULINE SIRKER: *(With French accent.)* I don't want candy. I want to see you.

NELLIE BLY, AGE 54: *(Continues to write.)* Indeed, I am a sight in this weather!

PAULINE SIRKER: My grammére says you were famous once.

NELLIE BLY, AGE 54: *(Chuckles, continues to write.)* It can happen to anyone, without the slightest warning or permission.

PAULINE SIRKER: You are ze American writer lady. You write about ze poor and misfortunate. You are Nellie Bly.

NELLIE BLY, AGE 54: *(Stops writing, looks up.)* Guilty on all counts. Sit here, dearie. *(Pats adjacent deck chair.)*

(Pauline Sirker sits on deck chair facing Nellie Bly.)

NELLIE BLY, AGE 54: What is your name?

PAULINE SIRKER: *Je m'appelle* Pauline Sirker. I am from Luxembourg. My father was killed in 1916 at Verdun.

NELLIE BLY, AGE 54: I'm sorry to hear that. My father also died when I was young. He didn't leave us much money, but oh, he left us a wonderful library full of the most glorious books!

(LIGHTS FADE OUT LEFT; LIGHTS UP RIGHT on NELLIE BLY, AGE 11 sitting cross-legged at down right and reading a book. SPOTLIGHT MID-RIGHT on BARBERSHOP QUARTET singing medium-tempo chorus of "Nelly Bly.")

BARBERSHOP QUARTET: *(Sings.)*
> Hey, Nellie! Ho, Nellie! Listen now to me!
> I'll sing for you, play for you, a dulcet melody!

(SPOTLIGHT OUT ON QUARTET; NELLIE'S MOTHER enters from right and sees Nellie.)

NELLIE'S MOTHER: Excuse me, young lady, but I've never heard of a pot scrubbed clean by reading about it!

NELLIE, AGE 11: *(Scrambles to her feet.)* Mother, this is the most exciting book! An adventure about Magellan sailing around the world! Did you know he met cannibals?

NELLIE'S MOTHER: I don't know where you get your imagination!

NELLIE, AGE 11: But, mother, this isn't my imagination. It's a fact, right here in this book!

NELLIE'S MOTHER: A girl your age should be more interested in housework than books.

NELLIE, AGE 11: Mother, I want to know the truth about things. I want to know how the world got the way it is, and I want to know why. And then I might just want to change it!

(SOUND OFFSTAGE RIGHT: baby crying.)

NELLIE'S MOTHER: Go change your baby sister's diaper. Then worry about changing the world!

(LIGHTS OUT LEFT as Nellie's Mother and Nellie, Age 11 exit right; SPOTLIGHT MID-RIGHT on Barbershop Quartet singing up-tempo verse of "Nelly Bly.")

BARBERSHOP QUARTET: *(Sings.)*
> Nellie Bly! Grown up now! Searching for the truth!
> Made her way to Old New York as fast as she could scoot!

(SPOTLIGHT OUT ON QUARTET; LIGHTS UP CENTER on NELLIE BLY, AGE 22 standing in front of desk at mid-center; sitting behind desk is JOSEPH PULITZER; sitting to left of desk is JOHN COCKERILL.)

JOHN COCKERILL: Miss Bly, the *New York World* must uphold the standards of contemporary journalism.

NELLIE BLY, AGE 22: Meaning, Mr. Cockerill, you won't hire a female reporter. Some editor you are!

JOHN COCKERILL: These stories you wrote for the paper in Pittsburgh…

NELLIE BLY, AGE 22: On divorce…

JOHN COCKERILL: Working women…

NELLIE BLY, AGE 22: Unsafe factory conditions…

JOHN COCKERILL: Economics of family life…

NELLIE BLY, AGE 22: I went to Mexico…

JOHN COCKERILL: You sent back recipes for tamales…

NELLIE BLY, AGE 22: And stories about corruption in Mexican politics! I was even deported!

JOHN COCKERILL: *(Sighs.)* You *are* an excellent writer…

NELLIE BLY, AGE 22: Mr. Pulitzer, the *New York World* is the most respected name in newspaper publishing. And you are its publisher.

JOSEPH PULITZER: I try to maintain a standard of fairness.

NELLIE BLY, AGE 22: How fair is it to not allow half the population of the country — women — a voice in your paper?

JOHN COCKERILL: *(Rises.)* Miss Bly, do you know to whom you are speaking?

NELLIE BLY, AGE 22: I do, sir. *(Leans on desk and looks Joseph Pulitzer in the eye.)* Joseph Pulitzer, the first national publisher who had the courage to hire a woman reporter.

JOSEPH PULITZER: You are extremely persistent.

JOHN COCKERILL: She's camped outside my office the last three days!

JOSEPH PULITZER: Very well, Miss Bly. Let us see if you truly have what it takes to write for the *World*. Cockerill, issue her a salary advance of twenty-five dollars. And good luck to you, Miss Bly. You will certainly need it on this assignment.

(LIGHTS OUT CENTER; SPOTLIGHT ON Nellie Bly, Age 54 and Pauline Sirker sitting at down left.)

NELLIE BLY, AGE 54: Mr. Pulitzer wasn't joking. My story was to expose the terrible conditions at the women's asylum on Blackwell's Island, in the East River. I pretended I was a crazy person, wandering the streets of New York with seventy-three cents in my pocket, until I was arrested and sent to the island.

PAULINE SIRKER: What happened then?

NELLIE BLY, AGE 54: *(Shudders.)* I almost don't want to recall.

(SPOTLIGHT OUT DOWN LEFT; SPOTLIGHT UP DOWN RIGHT ON Nellie Bly, Age 22 in a ragged dress standing, slumped, head lowered.)

ASYLUM WARDEN: *(O.S.)* Miss Brown!

(Nellie Bly does not move.)

ASYLUM WARDEN: *(O.S.)* Miss Brown!

(Nellie Bly does not move.)

ASYLUM WARDEN: *(O.S.)* Nurse!

(ASYLUM NURSE enters from right and prods Nellie Bly with a long straight stick; Nellie jumps to alertness and cringes away from Asylum Nurse, who stands nearby, ready to prod again.)

ASYLUM WARDEN: *(O.S.)* That's better. Miss Brown, you have been judged a danger to yourself and society. You will remain in Blackwell's Island Female Asylum until the doctors have pronounced your insanity cured.

NELLIE BLY, AGE 22: But I am not insane!

(Asylum Nurse threatens Nellie Bly with the stick, and Nellie cringes away.)

ASYLUM WARDEN: *(O.S.)* We will decide that, not you!

(Asylum Nurse exits right. SOUND: metal door slamming shut. LIGHTS FADE UP TO HALF to include area at down center, where an ASYLUM INMATE sits on floor, crying.)

NELLIE BLY, AGE 22: I'm sorry. I didn't know you were here.

ASYLUM INMATE: *(Looks up, laughs bitterly.)* Oh, I am *not* here! I have disappeared from the world! My family has been told I am dead! I may as well be!

NELLIE BLY, AGE 22: What is your name?

ASYLUM INMATE: Bridget. I think…or maybe it was Kathleen… *(Laughs.)* I can't remember any more!

NELLIE BLY, AGE 22: How long have you been here?

ASYLUM INMATE: A year, maybe two…oh, don't think *you'll* be leaving any time soon.

NELLIE BLY, AGE 22: But the doctors—

ASYLUM INMATE: Ha! The doctors aren't here to make you better, girl! They're here to make you worse!

(SOUND: metal door creaking open. ASYLUM DOCTOR enters from right, followed by Asylum Nurse, who carries a bucket.)

ASYLUM DOCTOR: I am Dr. Stone. Open your mouth, Miss Brown. *(Looks in Nellie Bly's mouth with tongue depressor.)* Say "aaahhh!"

NELLIE BLY, AGE 22: Aaahhh!

ASYLUM DOCTOR: Close your mouth, Miss Brown. *(Hands a pill to Nellie Bly.)* Take this pill. It will relieve your symptoms of anxiety. *(Turns to Asylum Inmate.)* Nurse, this one is dirty. Give her a bath.

ASYLUM INMATE: No, please!

(Asylum Inmate scrambles to her knees, but Asylum Doctor holds her down, pinning her hands behind her back as Asylum Nurse takes bucket

and dumps water over Asylum Inmate's head. SOUND: water splashing from bucket onto floor.)

ASYLUM INMATE: *(Screams.)* Noooooo!
NELLIE BLY, AGE 22: That water is freezing! She'll catch pneumonia!

(Asylum Doctor releases Asylum Inmate, who falls to floor in a heap, and walks toward right exit, followed by Asylum Nurse.)

ASYLUM DOCTOR: It will be your turn next, Miss Brown.

(Asylum Doctor and Asylum Nurse exit right. SOUND: metal door slamming shut. Nellie Bly crosses to Asylum Inmate, picks up a small thin blanket from floor and wraps it around the sobbing woman.)

NELLIE BLY, AGE 22: I'll make sure you aren't forgotten. Nor Dr. Stone, either.

(LIGHTS OUT RIGHT as Nellie Bly, Age 22 and Asylum Inmate exit right; NEWSIE enters from right, displaying newspaper headline "Behind Asylum Bars!" while crossing to exit left.)

NEWSIE: Extra, extra! Nellie Bly in Blackwell's Island! How the city's unfortunates are fed and treated! Cold baths and cruel nurses! *(exits)*

(SPOTLIGHT ON Nellie Bly, Age 54 and Pauline Sirker sitting at down left.)

NELLIE BLY, AGE 54: After ten days in that madhouse, I very nearly thought *I* was insane. But my editors arranged for my release, and I wrote a story exposing the dreadful conditions in the asylum. Many needed reforms were put in place.
PAULINE SIRKER: I suppose zat story made a lot of people very angry.
NELLIE BLY, AGE 54: It certainly did. But you can't make an omelette without breaking a few eggs.

(LIGHTS OUT LEFT; SPOTLIGHT MID-RIGHT on Barbershop Quartet singing up-tempo verse of "Nelly Bly.")

BARBERSHOP QUARTET: *(Sings.)*
> Nellie Bly! Riding high! Justice is her cry!
> Adventure calls, and she replies with a sparkle in her eye!

(SPOTLIGHT OUT ON QUARTET; LIGHTS UP CENTER on NELLIE BLY, AGE 22 standing in front of desk at mid-center; sitting behind desk is JOSEPH PULITZER; sitting to left of desk is JOHN COCKERILL.)

JOHN COCKERILL: Miss Bly, the *New York World* would never consider such a ludicrous stunt! We must uphold the standards of contemporary journalism.

NELLIE BLY, AGE 22: Meaning, Mr. Cockerill, you'll let your competition beat you to the punch. Some editor you are!

JOHN COCKERILL: But traveling around the world to beat the time of a fictional character!

NELLIE BLY, AGE 22: Phileas Fogg.

JOHN COCKERILL: In a fictional book!

NELLIE BLY, AGE 22: *Around the World in Eighty Days* by Jules Verne.

JOHN COCKERILL: By an author no one has heard of!

JOSEPH PULITZER: I've heard of Jules Verne.

JOHN COCKERILL: You have?

NELLIE BLY, AGE 22: Of course, he has.

JOSEPH PULITZER: And I think Miss Bly's idea of sending a reporter to trace Fogg's route around the world and beat his record of eighty days is an excellent idea.

JOHN COCKERILL: You do?

NELLIE BLY, AGE 22: Of course, he does.

JOSEPH PULITZER: Tell Frank Doherty to pack his bags and book passage right away.

NELLIE BLY, AGE 22: What?!?! You can't send Doherty! It was my idea!

JOHN COCKERILL: Miss Bly, a woman would not be safe traveling alone.

NELLIE BLY, AGE 22: No less safe than walking the streets of New York!

JOHN COCKERILL: A woman would also require many trunks full of clothes, hats, shoes, various accessories. Trying to make connections with all that luggage would be impossible!

NELLIE BLY, AGE 22: I'll fit everything I take in one case!

JOHN COCKERILL: Miss Bly—

NELLIE BLY, AGE 22: Or, I'll go to another paper and write the story for them!

JOHN COCKERILL: *(Rises.)* Miss Bly, do you know to whom you are speaking?

NELLIE BLY, AGE 22: I do, sir. *(Leans on desk and looks Joseph Pulitzer in the eye.)* Joseph Pulitzer, the first national publisher who had the courage to send a woman reporter around the world.

JOSEPH PULITZER: You are extremely persistent.

JOHN COCKERILL: *(Throws up his hands.)* Mercy!

JOSEPH PULITZER: Very well. Let us see if you truly have what it takes to go around the world in eighty days. Cockerill, issue her an expense advance of twenty-five hundred dollars in travel cheques. And good luck to you, Miss Bly. You will certainly need it on this assignment.

(LIGHTS OUT CENTER; SPOTLIGHT MID-RIGHT on Barbershop Quartet singing up-tempo chorus of "Nelly Bly.")

BARBERSHOP QUARTET: *(Sings.)*
Hey, Nellie! Ho, Nellie! Sailing cross the waves!
Reaching England's southern shore by just the seventh day!

(LIGHTS UP DOWN RIGHT as Nellie Bly, Age 22, stands at down right dressed in traveling outfit, writing in her notebook.)

NELLIE BLY, AGE 22: Left New York, morning of November 14, 1889, on the *Augusta Victoria*. Arrive in England and discover that Jules Verne himself wants to see me! I wish this train would move faster! There's not a minute to lose!

(As Barbershop Quartet sings, JULES VERNE enters from right, tips his hat, smiles and shakes hands with Nellie Bly.)

BARBERSHOP QUARTET: *(Sings.)*
Hey, Nellie! Ho, Nellie! France to Italy!
And then by ship along the Nile, oh what sights to see!

JULES VERNE: *(To audience.)* Miss Bly is the prettiest young girl imaginable. Even Madame Verne thinks so. Nobody — to look at the quiet, ladylike little thing — would have thought for a moment that she was what she is and that she was going to do what she is doing. Yet, I must say Nellie Bly looks built for hard work!

(SPOTLIGHT OUT ON QUARTET; Newsie enters from right, displaying newspaper headline "Nellie in Egypt!" while crossing to exit left.)

NEWSIE: Extra, extra, read all about it! Nellie Bly Goes to Land of Pharaohs! Read all about it! *(Exits.)*

(TWO EGYPTIAN SUITORS enter from right, bow to each other, stand on either side of Nellie Bly and bow to her.)

NELLIE BLY, AGE 22: *(Writing.)* The international traveler is guaranteed to meet the most curious people...

EGYPTIAN SUITOR #1: My dearest American flower of beatitude!

EGYPTIAN SUITOR #2: May I offer your hand to me in marriageship?

NELLIE BLY, AGE 22: I beg your pardon?

EGYPTIAN SUITOR #1: *(On knees.)* I have waited for you all of my life! Your refusal would destructify me!

EGYPTIAN SUITOR #2: *(Takes Nellie's hand.)* It would destructify me more!

EGYPTIAN SUITOR #1: *(Takes Nellie's other hand.)* Say you will be mine, O Majestic Breeze of the Swirling Desert!

EGYPTIAN SUITOR #2: *(Tugs Nellie's hand.)* Mine, O Delicate Firefly with Eyes of Fatal Enchantment!

NELLIE BLY, AGE 22: *(Pulls her hands away.)* Gentlemen! I am not entertaining marriage proposals from anyone! I am a reporter, and I am working! Oh, won't this boat go any faster? There's not a minute to lose!

(TWO EGYPTIAN SUITORS throw up their hands and exit left; before leaving, Egyptian Suitor #1 hands a stuffed monkey to Nellie Bly, Age 22.)

NELLIE BLY, AGE 22: But I *did* fall in love! While crossing the Arabian Sea to Ceylon, I met the most extraordinary young fellow! An East African monkey I named McGinty. He was the best company on the entire trip!

(SOUND: sea storm/wind noise; LIGHTS FLICKER AND DIM TO THREE-QUARTER.)

NELLIE BLY, AGE 22: *('To audience.)* Things suddenly took a turn for the worse. I waited in Ceylon five long days for a ship to Singapore. Thirty-three days into the race, and I was falling behind schedule! And then, on the voyage from Singapore to Hong Kong, disaster struck!

(SOUND: lightning crack; LIGHTS FLICKER. TWO SAILORS enter from right, mutter and point finger at Nellie while standing on either side of her.)

SAILOR #1: Ship taking water! We all die!
SAILOR #2: Monkey bad luck! Throw overboard!
NELLIE BLY, AGE 22: *(Recoils from Sailors.)* No! That's just a silly superstition!

(Sailors advance on Nellie, who stands her ground.)

SAILOR #1: Monkey very bad luck! Bring storm!
SAILOR #2: We all die! Must go overboard!

NELLIE BLY, AGE 22: If he goes overboard, I go, too!

(Sailors freeze as Nellie clutches monkey tightly. STORM SOUNDS STOP; LIGHTS UP FULL. Sailors relax, tip hats to Nellie, chuckle as they drift across stage to exit left.)

SAILOR #1: Storm stop. Ship all right.
SAILOR #2: We no die! Good!
SAILOR #1: Monkey cute!
SAILOR #2: Hi there, monkey!
SAILOR #1: Monkey good luck!
SAILOR #2: Bye-bye, monkey!

(Sailors exit left; Nellie tears off page from notebook and waves it in the air.)

NELLIE BLY, AGE 22: In Hong Kong I received the biggest shock of all — another woman was racing me around the world, traveling the opposite direction!

(Newsie enters from left, displaying newspaper headline "Gonged in Hong Kong!" while crossing to exit right.)

NEWSIE: Extra, extra, read all about it! Lizzie Bisland, editor at Cosmopolitan magazine, pulls ahead of Nellie Bly! Read all about it! *(Exits.)*
NELLIE BLY, AGE 22: I lost five precious days leaving Hong Kong! Finally, on the forty-ninth day, I got to Japan and there caught a berth to San Francisco on the *Oceanic*.

(CAPTAIN OF THE OCEANIC enters from right and addresses audience.)

CAPTAIN OF THE OCEANIC: Gentlemen, I am the Captain of the *Oceanic*. And as we traverse the white-capped foam of the blue

Pacific, we have but one thought in mind — For Nellie Bly, We'll Win or Die!

TWO SAILORS & TWO EGYPTIAN SUITORS: *(O.S.)* Hurrah! For Nellie Bly, We'll Win or Die!

(Sailor #1 enters from left, hands folded notepaper to Captain, who reads it.)

NELLIE BLY, AGE 22: But just before we arrived in San Francisco, there was a problem.

CAPTAIN OF THE OCEANIC: To get off the ship, we need our certificates of good health. By mistake, those were left in Japan.

NELLIE BLY, AGE 22: I have only eleven days to get to New York!

CAPTAIN OF THE OCEANIC: It will take two weeks for the papers to reach us.

NELLIE BLY, AGE 22: I am getting to shore if I have to jump in the water and swim there myself.

CAPTAIN OF THE OCEANIC: Hold your seahorses, Nellie! I've called a local doctor from the health department. Here he is now.

(HEALTH DEPARTMENT DOCTOR, nearsighted with glasses, enters from right; with a stethoscope in hand he listens to Sailor #1's elbow, Captain's ear and Nellie's monkey.)

HEALTH DEPARTMENT DOCTOR: My, that's a fine-looking baby you have there, madam!

(Sailor #2 enters from left, stands at down left and calls to Nellie.)

SAILOR #2: Miss Bly, your tugboat is waiting!

(Nellie crosses quickly to down left.)

NELLIE BLY, AGE 22: Thank you, Captain!

HEALTH DEPARTMENT DOCTOR: Wait a minute! I haven't checked your tongue!

(Nellie turns and sticks out her tongue, then exits left behind Sailor #2. Captain, Doctor, Sailor #1 exit right; SPOTLIGHT MID-RIGHT on Barbershop Quartet singing up-tempo verse of "Nelly Bly.")

BARBERSHOP QUARTET: *(Sings.)*
Nellie Bly! Won the race with eight days left to spare!
She's the Yankee Doodle Girl! No other can compare!

(SOUND: crowd cheers offstage. SPOTLIGHT OUT ON Barbershop Quartet. LIGHTS UP CENTER on John Cockerill and Joseph Pulitzer at desk.)

JOHN COCKERILL: On January 26, 1890, Nellie Bly arrived in Jersey City — seventy-two days after sailing from America on the *Augusta Victoria*. Thousands were on hand to greet her.

(Newsie enters from right and stands at down right, displaying newspaper headline "Father Time Outdone!")

NEWSIE: Extra, extra, read all about it! Nellie Bly most famous woman in the world!
JOSEPH PULITZER: Her name adorned pictures, advertisements and songs.
JOHN COCKERILL: Nellie Bly hats and coats became the fashion rage.
JOSEPH PULITZER: She wrote a best-selling book about her trip and was paid a salary of twenty-five thousand dollars a year — the highest of any reporter in the country.
NEWSIE: And the little monkey that traveled with her all the way from Egypt? She released him to the Central Park Zoo.

(LIGHTS OUT RIGHT AND CENTER; SPOTLIGHT ON on Nellie Bly, Age 54 and Pauline Sirker sitting at down left.)

NELLIE BLY, AGE 54: I married a few years later and lived a wonderful life with a wonderful man. After my husband died, I went to Austria the month before Sarajevo, and was trapped by the World

War. But, I made good use of bad luck and became the first woman
war correspondent.

PAULINE SIRKER: And now you are going back to America to write?

NELLIE BLY, AGE 54: That's what I do best, my dear. We made the
world safe for democracy. Now we have to make sure democracy
has a place at our own dinner table.

PAULINE SIRKER: I think I want to be a writer someday. Like you.

NELLIE BLY, AGE 54: *(Hands pencil and notebook to Pauline.)* Then
start writing, mademoiselle! And hurry! There's not a minute to lose!

*(SOUND OFFSTAGE: ocean liner horn sounds twice. LIGHTS
FADE TO BLACK. Barbershop Quartet sings slow-tempo chorus of
"Nelly Bly.")*

BARBERSHOP QUARTET: *(Sings.)*
Hey, Nellie! Ho, Nellie! She blazed a glory trail!
Her writing shone a guiding light that always will prevail!
Hey, Nellie! Ho, Nellie!

(LIGHTS OUT.)

THE END

Nelly Bly

**(music: Stephen Foster, words: Stephen Foster,
L.E. McCullough, arr. by L.E. McCullough)**

Nelly Bly, pg. 2

Nelly Bly, pg. 3

Nelly Bly, pg. 4

eight days left to spare! She's the Yan- kee Doo- dle Girl! No

bum- bum- bum

o- ther can com- pare! Hey, Nel- lie! Ho, Nel- lie! She blazed a glo- ry trail! Her

writ- ing shone a guid- ing light that al- ways will pre- vail! Hey, Nel- lie!

Ho, Nel- lie!

Nelly Bly, pg. 5

Marking Time:
Clocks and Calendars through the Centuries

Our everyday language is filled with references to time — "quality time," "hang time," "wait a sec," "in a New York minute," "time to rise and shine" — but it was only during the last two centuries that accurate measurement of time was possible and only within the last few decades that ordinary folks took to carrying timepieces as they went about their daily business. In some ways we take the mystery of time for granted; though it took humanity thousands of years to capture the endless flow of time in clocks and calendars and digital watches, one wonders if we have not now become servants of the machines we use to chart the progress of our lives to the nanosecond?

RUNNING TIME: 20 minutes

TIME: Late last night

PLACE: Cara's living room

CAST: 7 actors, min. 1 boy (•), 2 girls (+)
+ Cara, 12 going on 13   • T.F. (Tempus Fugit)
+ Mother (offstage)   4 Time Keepers

STAGE SET: sofa at mid center with a small end table adjacent

PROPS: wristwatch, 2 magazines, portable phone, tall glass of soda pop, magic marker, sand hourglass, candle, incense stick in bowl, small spice box

EFFECT: Sound — bell chimes

MUSIC: *Time Moves On; Bell Song*

COSTUMES: Cara wears contemporary pre-teen around-the-house casual clothes; T.F. wears a black suit or tux with a top hat emblazoned with a picture of a large hourglass; Time Keepers wear white leotard-type outfits or white t-shirts with white sweat pants decorated with magic-marker drawings of clock hands in various time positions

LIGHTS UP CENTER on CARA sitting at mid center on sofa; restless, she sips from a glass of soda pop and flips through a couple magazines before tossing them aside.

CARA: *(Checks her wristwatch.)* It's going to be my birthday in two hours! I can't wait! I just can't wait! *(Picks up a portable phone and dials.)* Shanice? Shanice, this is Cara, what are you wearing to my party tomor — who's this? Bob's All-Night Waffle Shack? Where's Shanice? No, I don't want any waffles! And I don't want any fries with the waffles I don't want! *(Clicks off, tosses phone aside.)*

MOTHER: (O.S) Cara! It's past your beddy-bye time!

CARA: Coming, Motherrrrrrrrr! *(To herself.)* When I'm thirteen, there won't *be* any more beddy-bye time for *this* girl! *(Fold arms, slumps back in sofa.)* I'll stay up as late as I want, when *ever* I want! *(Yawns.)* Come onnnnnnn, midnight! *(Gets comfortable in sofa, yawns.)* Why does time move so slow *(Yawns.)* when you want it to move fast? Mmmm…come onnnnnnn, midnight…*(Begins nodding off.)*

(LIGHTS FADE ALMOST TO BLACK.)

CARA: Come onnnnnnnnnnnnn…*(Falls asleep.)*

(LIGHTS STAY LOW FOR FIVE SECONDS, THEN FADE UP FULL AT CENTER; Cara jerks awake; her wristwatch is no longer on her arm.)

CARA: Midnight! *(Looks around.)* Wow, I must've fallen asleep. I bet it's midnight! It has to be! *(Looks at her wrist to check watch.)* Oh, no! My watch! Where is it? *(Jumps up, checks sofa, walks in a circle around sofa looking all around for watch.)* Here, watchie, here, watchie! I can't believe this! I *have* to know if I'm thirteen yet! *(Stops.)* Whoa, no panic. I can check the microwave in the kitchen. That has a timer.

(Cara runs to down left, peers at audience.)

CARA: That's wild! The microwave timer's not working. *(Presses a couple buttons.)* No, I don't want to defrost any tuna casserole! I want to know what time it is! Wait, the fax machine in mom's office!

(Cara runs to down right, peers at audience.)

CARA: Uh-oh…no date, no time? Computer! *(Moves a step forward, presses an "on" button.)* The computer has a clock. *(Peers closer.)* Huh? No time display? Must be having memory problems. Wait! The television and VCR! They've got clocks.

(Cara runs to down center, peers at audience.)

CARA: I do *not* believe this…all the clocks are gone! All the time is gone!

(SPOTLIGHT UP LEFT on T.F. standing at up left.)

T.F.: Hickory-dickory-dock! The mouse ran up the clock! And she took alllllll the time with her into the mouse hole!

(Cara whirls around.)

CARA: Excuse me, but Halloween was last month.

T.F.: Tempus Fugit is the name, keeping time is my game. *(Bows deeply with a flourish.)*

CARA: My brother has the weirdest friends! Eddie's gone camping this weekend, so you can just fly back to your — what did you say your name was?

T.F.: Tempus Fugit. *(Gives shorter bow, advances to sofa.)*

CARA: Hmmm. Isn't that a Latin phrase for "Time Flies?"

T.F.: Call me T.F. for short.

CARA: How about if I call 9-1-1? Look, Fugee, leave quietly, and I'll let you come to my birthday party tonight. Oh, no! What time is it?

T.F.: Time?

CARA: Quit kidding around! I have to know what time it is!

T.F.: Then we'd better call in the Time Keepers.

> *(FOUR TIME KEEPERS enter, Time Keepers #1 and #2 from left, Time Keepers #3 and #4 from right; as they cross to down center to flank T.F. and Cara, they sing "Time Moves On.")*

FOUR TIME KEEPERS: *(Sing.)*
> Time moves on and on and on
> Day and night and all year long
> When you sleep time marches by
> Leaving foot prints cross the sky

T.F: In the beginning of time…was time.
TIME KEEPER #1: Eons of time.
TIME KEEPER #2: Vast, unbroken seas of time.
T.F: The moon was the first measurement of time. People noticed it appeared at certain points in the sky at regular intervals.
TIME KEEPER #3: *(Points up.)* A new moon! We can plant our crops!
TIME KEEPER #4: *(Points up.)* A full moon! We can begin our hunt!
T.F: Early humans who farmed and hunted organized their activities around the cycles of the moon. These cycles were divided into seasons.
TIME KEEPER #1: The ancient Egyptians charted time by the course of the sun. They invented a calendar that had three hundred sixty-five days.
TIME KEEPER #2: Twelve months of thirty days each, with five extra days added on.
CARA: What did they do with the extra days?
T.F.: They danced!

> *(Time Keepers #3 and 4 dance with each other briefly.)*

TIME KEEPER #1: Many people marked a new month or new season with a festival celebrating the gods!
TIME KEEPER #2: *(Claps hands for dancers.)* Osiris! Bacchus! Chango! Athena!

T.F.: But a shorter unit of time was needed.

TIME KEEPER #1: The "week." A group of days that repeat in the same sequence.

TIME KEEPER #2: The ancient Greeks had no week.

TIME KEEPER #3: The Romans had a week of eight days, which they finally put to seven.

TIME KEEPER #4: Each day named after a different planet of the sky.

TIME KEEPER #1: Sun-day!

TIME KEEPER #2: Moon-day!

TIME KEEPER #3: Tuesday, for Mars.

TIME KEEPER #4: Wednesday, for Mercury.

TIME KEEPER #1: Thursday — Jupiter's Day.

TIME KEEPER #2: Friday — Day of Venus.

TIME KEEPER #3: And Saturn's Day — Saturday.

TIME KEEPER #4: But people needed to measure the passing of time *during* each day.

(Time Keeper #1 steps forward and stands stiffly straight, mimicing a sundial post.)

T.F.: It was noticed that the shadow of an upright stick became shorter as the sun rose in the sky…and longer as the sun set.

(Time Keeper #1 rotates slowly in a circle.)

TIME KEEPER #2: The sundial was created — a device that measured the path of the sun across the sky by keeping track of the sun's shadow.

CARA: But what good is a sundial if the sky is cloudy? Then there's no shadow!

TIME KEEPER #3: And the sun shines for different lengths at different times of the year.

TIME KEEPER #4: And in different places. A sundial measures a longer hour at the Equator than at the North or South Pole.

T.F.: Water, please.

CARA: Excuse me?

T.F.: I'd like some water, please. H_2O!

CARA: *(Hands him the glass of soda pop.)* Here's some Zingy Zowie Fruit Punch.

T.F.: Same difference! *(Holds glass aloft.)* Behold, the water clock!

TIME KEEPER #1: Drip. Drip. Drip. Drip. *(Continues under dialogue.)*

TIME KEEPER #2: By controlling the frequency of water dripping from one pot to another, the water clock could measure time in the *dark!*

TIME KEEPER #3: *(Marks levels on glass.)* By recording the decrease in water level, the passage of time could be measured in precise units.

TIME KEEPER #4: Except in winter, when water freezes.

TIME KEEPER #2: But water clocks were very good for short units of time.

TIME KEEPER #3: Such as how long a lawyer was allowed to speak in court.

TIME KEEPER #4: Or how long to boil an egg.

T.F.: But they were never altogether accurate. *(Sternly, to Time Keeper #1.)* And sometimes very annoying.

TIME KEEPER #1: *(Stops "dripping.")* Sorry.

TIME KEEPER #2: *(Displays sand hourglass.)* In the eighth century A.D. a monk in France is said to have invented the first sand clock, or hourglass.

TIME KEEPER #3: No worry about sand freezing up or evaporating!

TIME KEEPER #4: And it was portable. Columbus used a half-hour hourglass on his voyage to the Indies.

TIME KEEPER #1: *(Displays candle.)* In the ninth century, Alfred the Great, King of the Saxons, used a candle clock!

TIME KEEPER #2: When he was a fighting for the crown, he made a vow that if his kingship were restored, he would devote a full third of each day to the service of God.

TIME KEEPER #3: Alfred's candle clock was made of six twelve-inch candles, all the same thickness. Each candle lasted four hours, so—

CARA: So Alfred knew that two candles lasted for eight hours, or one-third of the day.

T.F.: Clever, those Saxons, eh what? Two hundred years later in China, a terrible drought dried up all the wells — no water for the water clocks!

TIME KEEPER #4: Voila! *(Displays incense stick in bowl.)* The Chinese invent the incense clock!

TIME KEEPER #1: A trail of incense was placed within a large seal that had marks telling the time. You told time by the point to where the fire had burned in the seal.

TIME KEEPER #2: And in the seventeenth century in France, a Monsieur de Villayer created the spice clock!

TIME KEEPER #3: *(Displays small spice box.)* An edible timepiece!

TIME KEEPER #4: A clock that worked in the dark!

TIME KEEPER #1: Instead of numbers indicating the hour, the clock had small boxes, each with a different spice.

TIME KEEPER #2: When Monsieur reached for the hour hand of the clock, it guided him to the appropriate box.

TIME KEEPER #3: *(Tastes spice in box, grimaces.)* Ugggh! Oregano!

TIME KEEPER #4: Five a.m.! Rise and shine!

(Four Time Keepers sing "Time Moves On" and swirl around sofa, returning to original places at end of song.)

FOUR TIME KEEPERS: *(Sing.)*
Time moves on and on and on
To and fro and then it's gone
Like the wind it whispers soft
As it disappears aloft

CARA: Okay, so people made all these elaborate clocks out of natural elements to measure time. But how did they know *what* to measure? Who decided what a minute was? Or how many were in an hour?

(Time Keeper #1 and Time Keeper #2 kneel on one knee at down center and raise their arms to form a circle.)

T.F.: Behold, the circle! The ancient Egyptians divided the circle into three hundred sixty equal parts, or degrees, in order to chart the course of the sun traveling across the sky.

TIME KEEPER #3: *(Jumps through circle.)* They loved symmetry!

CARA: And their basic calendar had three hundred sixty days plus five extra.

TIME KEEPER #4: *(Jumps through circle.)* The number sixty was one-sixth of three hundred sixty.

TIME KEEPER #3: *(Jumps through circle.)* In Latin, the word "minuta" means a "small part" and stood for one-sixtieth of a unit.

TIME KEEPER #4: *(Jumps through circle.)* Thus, one-sixtieth of an hour!

TIME KEEPER #3: *(Jumps through circle.)* Our word "second" also comes from a Latin word, "secundae," which became one-sixtieth of a minute.

TIME KEEPER #4: *(Jumps through circle.)* But it wasn't until 1330 A.D. — at the dawn of the European Renaissance — that the modern hour became accepted as one of twenty-four equal parts of a day.

T.F.: For the first time in the history of time, the "day" included all the hours of the "night."

(Time Keeper #1 and Time Keeper #4 rise and stand at attention facing audience; Time Keeper #2 mimes pulling a bell rope that "sounds" Time Keeper #1; Time Keeper #3 mimes wielding a gong-beater that "sounds" Time Keeper #4.)

TIME KEEPER #1: *(Loudly.)* Ding—

TIME KEEPER #4: *(Loudly.)* Dong.

TIME KEEPER #1: *(Loudly.)* Ding—

TIME KEEPER #4: *(Loudly.)* Dong.

(Time Keepers continue sounding bells as Cara and T.F. shout above the din.)

CARA: *(Holding her ears.)* What is that noise?

T.F.: It's the sound of the first real clocks.

CARA: The what?

T.F.: The first clocks didn't have hands or even dials. They simply had to sound the hour.

CARA: What?

T.F.: The first real clocks as we know them were created in the Middle Ages for churches to call the faithful to prayer. Later, the bell moved into the public square and became a community news bulletin.

TIME KEEPER #2: Bells sounded fire alarms.

TIME KEEPER #1: *(Less loudly.)* Ding—

TIME KEEPER #3: Warned of an approaching army.

TIME KEEPER #4: *(Less loudly.)* Dong.

TIME KEEPER #2: Announced the birth of a king.

TIME KEEPER #1: *(Less loudly.)* Ding—

TIME KEEPER #3: Called people to the town fair.

TIME KEEPER #4: *(Less loudly.)* Dong.

CARA: Why didn't they just call a clock a bell?

T.F.: They did. Ever hear someone play a glockenspiel?

CARA: Sure! You hit the metal slabs with a mallet, and it sounds just like…like a bell!

T.F.: The English word "clock" comes from the German word "glocke," or "bell." Six hundred years ago a clock wasn't a clock unless it rang a bell, and every town worth its salt had plenty of bells. Remember your Mother Goose?

TIME KEEPER #1: *(Sings.)* Two sticks in an apple, say the bells of Whitechapel.

TIME KEEPER #2: *(Sings.)* Kettles and pans, say the bells of St. Ann's.

TIME KEEPER #3: *(Sings.)* Brickbats and tiles, say the bells of St. Giles.

TIME KEEPER #4: *(Sings.)* Old shoes and slippers, say the bells of St. Peter's.

FOUR TIME KEEPERS: *(Sing.)* Pokers and tongs, say the bells of St. John's.

T.F.: *(Applauds.)* Isn't that grand harmony! Too bad clocks in the Middle Ages weren't as harmonious as the choirs.

CARA: You mean a clock in London didn't tell the same time as a clock in Paris?

T.F.: A clock in your kitchen didn't tell the same time as a clock in your parlor. They weren't synchronized, and they weren't accurate.

TIME KEEPER #1: One day in the year 1583, the great Italian inventor Galileo sat in church daydreaming, as usual.

TIME KEEPER #2: *(Staring upward.)* He took to watching the altar lamp swing back and forth, back and forth…

TIME KEEPER #3: *(Staring upward.)* And noticed, by checking against his pulse, that the time it took the lamp to swing from one end to the other…

TIME KEEPER #4: Was the same.

T.F.: Galileo had discovered the first principle of the "pendulum effect," which is that the time it takes a pendulum to swing back and forth is governed by the *length* of the pendulum, *not* the width of its swing.

CARA: So people could set their clocks to the same time?

T.F.: Precisely. After that breakthrough, it became easier and easier to capture time and make it work for you. In the 1670s Robert Hooke and Christiaan Huygens invented a spring that could drive a clock, instead of depending on gravity.

TIME KEEPER #1: The first wristwatch was made in 1790 by two Swiss gentlemen, Droz and Leschot.

TIME KEEPER #2: The Englishman John Harwood patented the first self-winding watch in 1924.

TIME KEEPER #3: He also invented the first electric watch a few years later.

TIME KEEPER #4: And in 1961 the first fully electronic watch using a mercury cell was patented by the Bulova Company in the United States.

T.F.: As the devices for measuring and telling time became smaller and smaller, the importance of being "on time" grew larger and larger. The human species became obsessed with time, controlling time, defying time! *(Crosses to exit right.)*

(Time Keepers circle around Cara, speaking to her rapidly. SOUND: twelve bell chimes sound.)

TIME KEEPER #1: What time do you have?

TIME KEEPER #2: Two minutes fourteen seconds left in the quarter.

TIME KEEPER #3: Hurry, or you'll miss the ten-oh-five!

TIME KEEPER #4: Can I buy this sweater on time?

T.F.: Tempus fugit! *(Stands at down right.)*

TIME KEEPER #1: We made good time between Santa Fe and Shelbyville.

TIME KEEPER #2: Punch your time cards, please!

TIME KEEPER #3: Give me a minute, will you!

TIME KEEPER #4: Not a second to spare!

CARA: Time out!

(LIGHTS OUT; T.F. exits right; Time Keepers exit left. LIGHTS FADE UP CENTER on Cara alone on stage, lying on sofa, asleep and waking slowly, squinting at audience.)

CARA: Must be almost morning. Morning…*(jerks fully awake)* Yow! Morning! It's definitely past midnight. So I *must* be thirteen! Yes! *(Jumps up.)*

MOTHER: (O.S): Cara! It's time to get ready for school!

CARA: Coming, Motherrrrrrrr! *(To herself.)* Oh well, I probably have time for some hot chocolate. *(Looks at her wrist to check watch.)* Ohmygosh! My watch is here! Mom, my watch is here! Hey, of course, it's here! It's *always* here, right on my wrist.

MOTHER: (O.S): Are you up yet, Cara? Time flies!

CARA: I know, I know, tempus fugit. Wait a minute, what did I just say? Why am I speaking Latin? Never mind. Where's the phone? I've *got* to call Shanice! *(Searches sofa for phone.)* Tell her about that crazy dream, Time Beepers! Too wild! *(Pauses, pulls up something from under sofa pillow.)* Uh-oh! *(Displays a sand hourglass.)* I am *so* not ready for school today!

(LIGHTS FADE OUT as Four Time Keepers sing "Time Moves On" offstage.)

FOUR TIME KEEPERS: *(Sings, O.S.)*
   Time moves on and on and on
   Centuries pass as decades yawn
   Feel the present fading fast
   Catch the future streaming past

THE END

Time Moves On

(words & music by L.E. McCullough)

Time moves on and on and on; day and night and all year long;

When you sleep time mar- ches by leav- ing foot prints cross the sky

Bell Song

(words traditional, music by L.E. McCullough)

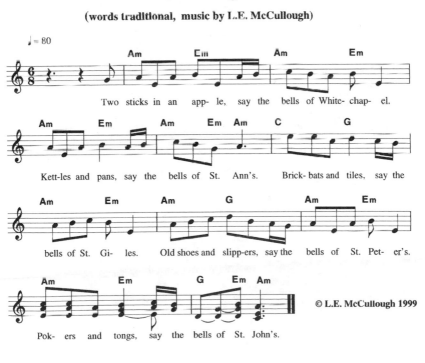

Two sticks in an app- le, say the bells of White- chap- el.

Kett-les and pans, say the bells of St. Ann's. Brick- bats and tiles, say the

bells of St. Gi- les. Old shoes and slipp-ers, say the bells of St. Pet- er's.

Pok- ers and tongs, say the bells of St. John's.

Isaac Newton's Poetry of the Rainbow

The English astronomer, mathematician and philosopher Isaac Newton (1642–1727) was the first Western scientist to win widespread admiration among his peers while still alive. Earlier pioneers in science had struggled against rigid intellectual establishments that feared new ideas; some scientists were imprisoned and put to death, others were simply ridiculed or ignored. Newton, however, lived in a time when science was beginning to be recognized for its useful applications to everyday life. Newton's discoveries helped put scientific inquiry on a practical footing leading to breakthroughs in many fields, and he received numerous honors including election to Parliament, appointment as Master of the Mint, President of the Royal Society and, at age 62, knighthood from the Queen — the first knighting ever granted for scientific achievement. At his death, he was regarded as a national hero.

RUNNING TIME: 15 minutes

TIME: April 4, 1727

PLACE: Westminster Abbey, London, England

CAST: 7 actors, min. 4 boys (•), 3 girls (+)

- Isaac Newton
- Voltaire
+ 3 Bystanders

- Malcolm Scribblesheet
- Alexander Pope

STAGE SET: scrim or white sheet at back of stage

PROPS: pencil (antique), notepad (antique), small prism, apple, Newton's cradle (a device with five metal balls on strings attached to a wood or metal frame)

EFFECTS: Sound — noise of a crowded hall filled by many people talking; Visual — projection of a prism rainbow on back wall

COSTUMES: All characters dress in early 18th-century urban attire befitting their occupation and social status — Voltaire and Alexander Pope as upperclass gentlemen with ruffled lace collars and sleeves, colorful jackets and vests, gaudy breeches, buckled shoes, powdered wigs; Isaac Newton as a more somberly-dressed version of Voltaire and Pope with dark frock, vest and breeches, white shirt, simple dark shoes and a late-17th-century shoulder-length wig; Malcolm Scribblesheet as a more common clerk with coarse shirt, dark vest and breeches, no coat; Three Bystanders as upperclass ladies with long, wide dresses, hair piled high with exotic combs, Bystander #1 carries a parasol, Bystander #2 carries a hand fan, Bystander #3 carries a covered basket from which she takes the Newton's cradle

SOUND: noise of a crowded hall filled by many people talking as LIGHTS FADE UP FULL on MALCOLM SCRIBBLESHEET standing at down center; he holds a short pencil and writes on a notepad, then pauses and reads what he has written. SOUND: crowd noise subsides.

MALCOLM SCRIBBLESHEET: Fourth of April, 1727. The scene inside Westminster Abbey, where the cream of English nobility lie entombed, can best be described as reverent, yet tempered with the bustling exultation of the concert hall or ship dock. Dukes and duchesses abound, even the Lord Chancellor attends. For this is not the funeral of any ordinary man…it is the laying to rest of a scientist renowned the world over — Sir Isaac Newton.

(VOLTAIRE enters from left, stands musing at down left.)

VOLTAIRE: He is buried like a king who had done well by his subjects.
MALCOLM SCRIBBLESHEET: It is the French philosopher Voltaire!

(Malcolm Scribblesheet crosses to Voltaire.)

MALCOLM SCRIBBLESHEET: Good day, Monsieur. Malcolm Scribblesheet, correspondent for the London Tattler-Dispatch. You were an admirer of Sir Isaac?
VOLTAIRE: Before Newton, all men were blind. A genius such as Isaac Newton is born once in a thousand years!
MALCOLM SCRIBBLESHEET: Would you say he was well thought of by his scientific peers?
VOLTAIRE: Isaac Newton lived into his eighties, happy and honored in his own country. Galileo ended his days persecuted by the Inquisition and Descartes died in exile and poverty. Before Newton, scientists were assumed to be in league with Lucifer. After Newton, they have become acclaimed as national treasures! *(Returns to musing pose.)*

(ALEXANDER POPE enters from right, stands at down right and declaims to audience as Voltaire exits left.)

ALEXANDER POPE: Nature, and Nature's Laws lay hid in night. God said, "Let Newton be!" and All was Light.

MALCOLM SCRIBBLESHEET: And there is the great English poet Alexander Pope! Mr. Pope!

(Malcolm Scribblesheet crosses to Pope.)

MALCOLM SCRIBBLESHEET: Love your rhymes, Mr. Pope. What would you say the major contribution of Isaac Newton has been — from the poet's perspective — to the field of science?

ALEXANDER POPE: Newton sought to explain the universe by means of physical laws expressed in mathematical form.

MALCOLM SCRIBBLESHEET: But that doesn't rhyme!

ALEXANDER POPE: All nature is but art, unknown to thee; all chance, direction, which thou cannot see. In a nutshell, my boy, Newton found poetry in the rainbow.

(Pope exits right as Malcolm Scribblesheet writes; THREE BYSTANDERS enter from left, strolling to down center and talking among each other.)

MALCOLM SCRIBBLESHEET: "Poetry of the rainbow." That's exquisite, Mr. Pope, it truly is. Now, what would you say — *(Looks up, notices Pope has left.)* Here come some bystanders. Let's hear what they have to say.

BYSTANDER #1: Very humble origins, you know. Born Christmas Day, 1642, in Woolsthorpe, a very small town in Lincolnshire. Father died before he was born and mother remarried but left little Isaac in care of the granny.

BYSTANDER #2: He went to a plain country grammar school but his mother brought him home at eleven to run the family farm. Fortunately, his uncle recognized the boy was better at calculating numbers than dragging a plow, so Isaac entered Cambridge at age nineteen. Being of humble means, he worked his way through school as a sort of man-servant to the wealthier students.

BYSTANDER #3: It was during these university years that he laid the foundation for his later experiments with studies in optics, physics and philosophy.

(ISAAC NEWTON enters from left displaying a prism; he stands at down left and speaks to audience.)

ISAAC NEWTON: In the year 1666, I procured a triangular glass prism. Having darkened my chamber and made a small hole in the window shuts to let in a convenient quantity of sunlight, I placed my prism so that it might be thereby refracted to the opposite wall.

(EFFECT: projection of a prism-refracted rainbow on back wall.)

ISAAC NEWTON: It was at first a very pleasing divertisement, to view the vivid and intense colors produced thereby. But after awhile, I became surprised to see them in an oblong form. By the existing Laws of Refraction, they should have been circular!

BYSTANDER #1: Newton came to learn that light is a mixture of several different parts.

BYSTANDER #2: Instead of the old idea that all colors were variations of white light, Newton put forth the idea that white light was itself a combination of all colors.

BYSTANDER #3: What Newton really proved was that such vague things as light and color could be described in precise measurements.

BYSTANDER #1: He had created a method of experimental process.

BYSTANDER #2: A process that led to new ways of describing basic principles of how things worked.

BYSTANDER #3: Instead of guessing at the causes of things, Newton showed how to go about looking for patterns. Or "properties."

(Projection fades.)

MALCOLM SCRIBBLESHEET: And then there was that bit about the apple falling on his head!

ISAAC NEWTON: A short while after graduating from Cambridge, I went back to the farm for a visit. I had much on my mind, and a spot in the country always refreshed me. One warm summer afternoon, I went to the orchard where I had often gone as a boy to be alone with my thoughts. While sitting in the shade of a favorite apple tree, near to dozing, I heard a *thump!* at my feet. *(Takes apple from his jacket and displays it.)* An apple had fallen. A trifling incident, but it set my mind whirling.

(Isaac Newton crosses to down center and tosses apple to Bystander #3.)

ISAAC NEWTON: Why should the apple always descend straight to the ground? Why not sideways, or upwards, but constantly to the earth's center?

(Bystander #3 tosses apple to Bystander #2.)

ISAAC NEWTON: Assuredly, because the earth draws the apple to itself. And what is this drawing power in the earth?

(Bystander #2 tosses apple to Bystander #1.)

ISAAC NEWTON: If matter draws matter, it must be in proportion of its quantity. The apple, therefore, draws the earth as well as the earth draws the apple. *(Takes the apple from Bystander #1.)* And this power is called Gravity, which extends itself throughout the entire universe. *(Takes a bite of apple.)*

(THREE BYSTANDERS applaud as Isaac Newton steps back to down left.)

BYSTANDER #1: Isn't it he brilliant!
BYSTANDER #2: And well-spoken!
BYSTANDER #3: Does he eat and sleep? Is he like other men?

ISAAC NEWTON: *(Bows, addresses Bystanders.)* I do not know what I may appear to be to the world, but to myself I seem to have been only like a boy playing on the seashore and diverting myself in now and then finding a smoother pebble or a prettier shell than ordinary, while the great ocean of truth lay all undiscovered before me. If I have seen further, it is only by standing on the shoulders of giants.

MALCOLM SCRIBBLESHEET: Didn't he put his theories about gravity and motion into a book that astounded the scientific establishment?

BYSTANDER #1: In 1687 Newton published his master work, *Mathematical Principles of Natural Philosophy.*

BYSTANDER #2: He stated three laws that all physical objects must obey.

ISAAC NEWTON: First, that a body will rigidly maintain its state of uniform motion in a straight line, or its state of rest, unless acted upon by an impressed force.

BYSTANDER #3: The law of inertia.

BYSTANDER #1: Like the first law, his second law was influenced by earlier research of Galileo.

ISAAC NEWTON: Second, all forces cause acceleration. If a force is doubled, so is the acceleration.

BYSTANDER #2: He reached his third law by studying how objects collide.

ISAAC NEWTON: For every action, there is an equal and opposite reaction.

BYSTANDER #3: *(Takes Newton's cradle from basket, displays it.)* As illustrated by this delightful toy.

MALCOLM SCRIBBLESHEET: Newton's cradle!

(LIGHTS FADE SLOWLY TO BLACK AS SPOTLIGHT SHINES ON Isaac Newton at down left.)

BYSTANDER #1: Alas, his fertile mind is stilled.

BYSTANDER #2: He was a scientist and a poet.

BYSTANDER #3: Searching for the poetry of the rainbow.

ISAAC NEWTON: And to those who say science in its explorations would destroy the poetry of the rainbow, I reply that I have simply drawn back the veil from the Almighty Hand that writes it.

(LIGHTS OUT.)

THE END

Naming the Unnamed:
The Strange Saga of Amerigo Vespucci

Amerigo Vespucci (1454–1512) was born in Florence, Italy, of a noble family during the height of the Italian Renaissance. As a young man Vespucci read widely, was trained in mathematics and collected maps and books on cosmography and astronomy. He entered the service of the Medicis, a prominent political and banking family who sent him to Spain in 1492 to look after their business. There Vespucci developed an original and remarkably accurate method of calculating longitude when navigating on the ocean by comparing the hour of the moon's conjunction with a planet observed at sea and the hour it was observed in Spain. After the publication of his voyage reports established his renown as an explorer, Vespucci was named Pilot-Major of Spain by Queen Joanna and founded a school for sea pilots. In view of the controversy over the naming of the New World that occurred in later years, it is ironic that Christopher Columbus (1451–1506) and Vespucci were friends in real life; Columbus died before the publication of the book naming the New World after Vespucci.

RUNNING TIME: 20 minutes

TIME: 1545

PLACE: Library of a country house near London, England

CAST: 14 actors, min. 9 boys (•), 5 girls (+)
+ Elizabeth, Age 12
• Amerigo Vespucci
• Christopher Columbus
• Gonçalo Coelho
+ King's Chamberlain
+ Scholar
+ Farmer

• Edward, Age 8
• Old Spanish John, Age 56
• Young Spanish John, Age 12
• King Manuel of Portugal
• Gauthier Lud
• Martin Waldseemüller
+ Merchant

STAGE SET: 2 stuffed or ornately-carved wooden chairs and a small table at down right (table has a globe of the world set on it); stool at down left; throne at mid-center

PROPS: 2 hardback books, world globe, basket of flowers, parchment paper, quill pen, scrolled map, astrolabe*

COSTUMES: All characters dress as 16th-century Europeans — men and boys wear basic outfit of black, brown or dark blue tights, black or brown pointed slippers or cloth shoes with buckles, ruffled or bloused white shirt with a jerkin-style jacket (hip-length, collarless, sleeveless, leather); characters of higher social station wear more accessories, hats, jewelry, a cloak, etc.; King Manuel should wear a crown; Elizabeth wears a dress, not especially ornate but with some jewelry and accessories

* The *astrolabe* was an instrument used at the turn of 16th century for measuring the altitude of the sun and stars. You could build a cardboard replica by fabricating a circle 12 inches in circumference with two cross-bars intersecting in the middle; at the middle intersection is fixed an arm that spins; a small ring is at the top

Stage Plan —*Naming the Unnamed: The Strange Saga of Amerigo Vespucci*

Key:　globe table　　throne

stool　　chair

An Astrolabe

LIGHTS UP RIGHT on EDWARD and ELIZABETH sitting in chairs at down right; each has a book in their lap.

EDWARD: I don't care what your tutor says, Elizabeth — you are wrong.

ELIZABETH: I am *not*.

EDWARD: Just because I am younger than you—

ELIZABETH: Doesn't mean you know who discovered America!

EDWARD: Very well, dear sister who is a fount of all geographic knowledge in the Year 1545. If, as you say, Columbus discovered America, why is America not called Columbia?

ELIZABETH: Because, well, because, because…it's quite simple, you see—

EDWARD: Yessssss?

ELIZABETH: Edward, you are annoying me greatly!

EDWARD: When I am king, Elizabeth, I shall annoy you even more!

(Elizabeth squeezes book shut and rises; she turns and spies OLD SPAN-ISH JOHN, who has entered from left carrying a basket of flowers, crossing to down center.)

ELIZABETH: There's Old Spanish John. We'll ask him.

EDWARD: He's only a gardener. What would he know of history and exploration?

ELIZABETH: Sir! Would you come here a moment?

(Old Spanish John stops, looks quizzically at the children.)

OLD SPANISH JOHN: *Sí, señor* Eduardo *y señorita* Elizabeth. I have some pretty flowers — *floras lindas.* See how pretty? *(Shows basket to Elizabeth.)*

ELIZABETH: I don't want to talk about floras, er, flowers.

EDWARD: She wants to talk about America. Have you heard of it, old chap? *(Chuckles.)* It's that rather large chunk of forest a bit to the west of Plymouth. *(Chuckles.)*

ELIZABETH: I want to know — who discovered the New World? Columbus? Or Vespucci?

(Old Spanish John hands the basket to Edward and crosses to globe.)

OLD SPANISH JOHN: It is good for children to be curious. I was curious as a boy, many years ago. So curious that I left my home in Seville and traveled to Portugal, to the port of Lisbon, where the greatest explorers of the age sailed off into glory — Columbus, da Gama, Magellan, Diaz. In 1501, I sailed as a cabin boy on an expedition to the newfound lands. The captain was Gonçalo Coelho, the pilot...Amerigo Vespucci.

(Old Spanish John spins the globe; LIGHTS FADE DOWN RIGHT; LIGHTS UP LEFT as AMERIGO VESPUCCI and GONÇALO COELHO enter from left and cross to down left, followed by YOUNG SPANISH JOHN; Coelho sits on the stool, facing audience; Vespucci carries an astrolabe and looks skyward, making longitude calculations which Young Spanish John writes on a piece of paper.)

GONÇALO COELHO: We have followed this coast a long ways, Pilot.
AMERIGO VESPUCCI: That is correct, Captain. According to my calculations, we have journeyed nearly eight hundred leagues. *(To Young Spanish John.)* Twenty-eight degrees west.
YOUNG SPANISH JOHN: *(Writes.)* Twenty-eight degrees west.
GONÇALO COELHO: Do you think we will indeed find the passage to the Moluccas, the El Dorado of spices?
AMERIGO VESPUCCI: If the passage exists anywhere, it cannot be far from here. We shall find it.
GONÇALO COELHO: But Columbus believes these are nothing more than islands off the coast of India and China.
AMERIGO VESPUCCI: My Italian colleague is very firm in his beliefs. But don't you think eight hundred leagues is a very long island, Captain?
GONÇALO COELHO: My brother was with Columbus on his second voyage. He made the crew swear an oath that Cuba is part of the

Chinese mainland. He even wrote Queen Isabella that "only a chan-
nel separates us from the Malay Peninsula...it is no further from
Panama to the Ganges than from Pisa to Genoa."

AMERIGO VESPUCCI: What he does not realize is that there are not
one, but *two* oceans between Europe and Asia. *(To Young Spanish
John.)* Thirty-four degrees south. Yes, Captain, Christopher
Columbus knows how to dream, but only a mathematician knows
how to make that dream a reality.

YOUNG SPANISH JOHN: What do you believe *we* have discovered,
Señor Vespucci?

AMERIGO VESPUCCI: *(Points toward audience.)* Juan Gomez, you
are looking at a *mundus novus* — a New World. A fourth continent that rivals Africa, Europe and Asia in size and wonder.

YOUNG SPANISH JOHN: But how is that possible, Captain? This
land is found on no maps.

AMERIGO VESPUCCI: *(Holds up astrolabe.)* We are making new
maps, muchacho. With every measurement you write, we shape a
New World!

*(LIGHTS FADE DOWN LEFT as AMERIGO VESPUCCI and
GONÇALO COELHO exit left; LIGHTS UP CENTER on the
KING MANUEL OF PORTUGAL at mid-center sitting on a throne;
the KING'S CHAMBERLAIN stands to the King's left reading from
papers.)*

OLD SPANISH JOHN: *(O.S.)* Vespucci's diary of the voyage was sent
directly to his patron, the King of Portugal.

KING'S CHAMBERLAIN: Vespucci then continues to describe the
marriage customs of the natives, including their childbirth, religion,
architecture, even their diet.

KING MANUEL: Remarkable, truly remarkable. I have never heard
a voyage account so detailed and poetically written.

KING'S CHAMBERLAIN: The man *is* a Florentine scholar, Your
Majesty.

KING MANUEL: Then we should produce such scholars in Portugal,
chamberlain! Pray, continue.

KING'S CHAMBERLAIN: "What should I tell of the multitude of wild animals, the abundance of pumas, of panthers, of wild cats, not like those of Iberia, but of the antipodes; of so many wolves, red deer, monkeys and felines, marmosets of many kinds, and many large snakes? Sailing along the coast, we discovered each day an endless number of people with various languages."

KING MANUEL: Indeed!

KING'S CHAMBERLAIN: "None of these countries were known to our ancestors. I have found a continent, more populous and more full of animals than our Europe, or Asia or Africa, and even more temperate than any other region known to us."

KING MANUEL: Most excellent! Have these diaries printed and bound for the royal library.

(Young Spanish John enters from left dressed as a court page.)

KING'S CHAMBERLAIN: Yes, Your Majesty. Page! Come hither!

YOUNG SPANISH JOHN: *(Bows.)* Sire.

(King's Chamberlain hands papers to Young Spanish John.)

KING'S CHAMBERLAIN: To the Royal Printer, boy. Quickly and let no eyes other than your own be their witness!

YOUNG SPANISH JOHN: *(Bows.)* Yes, sire. *(Turns, sticks papers inside his jacket, grins and dashes off left.)*

KING MANUEL: An abundance of pumas, of panthers…certainly an abundance of gold!

(LIGHTS OUT CENTER as King Manuel and King's Chamberlain exit up right.)

OLD SPANISH JOHN: *(O.S.)* However, it would seem that the young page *did* allow a section of Vespucci's diary to find other eyes. In 1504, in Paris and Florence, a small booklet written in Latin appears by an unknown author. It contains a report from one Albericus Vespucius about his voyage across the Western ocean. The booklet circulates throughout Europe, is quoted at fairs and universities, in letters from friends to business associates to diplomats. It is titled *Mundus Novus* — the New World.

(LIGHTS UP LEFT on CHRISTOPHER COLUMBUS sitting, hunched over, on stool at down left.)

FARMER: *(O.S.)* This Vespucius says Columbus discovered not a series of islands, but a continent.

SCHOLAR: *(O.S.)* Columbus' geography is nonsense! Vespucius is a mapmaker and a mathematician.

MERCHANT: *(O.S.)* A New World…new ports for trade…new sources of treasure…

OLD SPANISH JOHN: *(O.S.)* A few months before he died, Christopher Columbus wrote a letter to his son, Diego.

CHRISTOPHER COLUMBUS: I have spoken recently with Amerigo Vespucci, a countryman of mine, who is on his way to Court, where he is to be consulted on several points connected with navigation. He has at all times shown the desire to be pleasant to me. He is an honest man. And, though his efforts have not brought him the reward he might by rights to have expected, he is going to Court with the sincere desire to obtain something favorable for me. He has decided to do all in his power on my behalf. *(Calls offstage left.)* Juanito!

YOUNG SPANISH JOHN: *(Enters from left, bows.)* Señor Columbo.

CHRISTOPHER COLUMBUS: Deliver this…*(Coughs.)* to…*(Coughs, slumps.)*

YOUNG SPANISH JOHN: I will do as you wish, señor. *(Bows, exits left.)*

(LIGHTS OUT LEFT; Christopher Columbus exits left.)

OLD SPANISH JOHN: *(O.S.)* In 1504, Vespucci's fame as an explorer is spread further when his reports appear in a collection of travel writings published in Venice, again without his knowledge. In 1507, another travel book is published…a printer makes a mistake and leaves out the name of Columbus, so the title page reads: "New World and Countries Newly Discovered by Alberico Vespucci." But, the strangest turn of all is about to occur that same year in a remote village in the Duchy of Lorraine, when a French printer, Gauthier Lud, and a German mapmaker, Martin Waldseemüller, meet to plan a new book.

(LIGHTS UP LEFT on GAUTHIER LUD standing at down left; MARTIN WALDSEEMÜLLER sitting on stool, holding a scrolled map.)

GAUTHIER LUD: Monsieur Waldseemüller, we have a chance to make the Duke very, very happy.

MARTIN WALDSEEMÜLLER: Duke René is a wonderful patron of the arts. He has turned our small town of Saint-Dié into an oasis of the arts.

GAUTHIER LUD: Yes, and we must find a way to repay his generosity. This book on geography we had planned to print—

MARTIN WALDSEEMÜLLER: Yes?

GAUTHIER LUD: We should dedicate it to the Duke.

MARTIN WALDSEEMÜLLER: Yes!

GAUTHIER LUD: We must show the Duke is an important man.

MARTIN WALDSEEMÜLLER: Yes?

GAUTHIER LUD: What better way than to have these letters from Amerigo Vespucci addressed to the Duke as well as the King of Portugal?

MARTIN WALDSEEMÜLLER: Yes!

GAUTHIER LUD: Can you say something besides "yes?"

MARTIN WALDSEEMÜLLER: Yes! I mean, no! I mean, yes! No! Yes!

GAUTHIER LUD: Make a new map, monsieur. And write of the New World — "since Americus found it, may from now on be called the Earth of Americus, or America."

MARTIN WALDSEEMÜLLER: Yes! I mean, yes! Yes! Yes!

(LIGHTS FADE OUT LEFT as Waldseemüller opens map scroll and Lud exits left.)

OLD SPANISH JOHN: *(O.S.)* Martin Waldseemüller drew a map of the new land and labeled it America. From thence forth, the name flew from book to book, eye to eye, mouth to mouth, as the idea of a New World captured the imaginations of farmers, scholars and merchants throughout Europe.

(LIGHTS UP CENTER on Farmer, Scholar and Merchant sitting and standing at mid-center.)

FARMER: I have heard of many wondrous crops in America. Famines will be a thing of the past!

SCHOLAR: The continent of America will expand the horizons of man's knowledge. God's miracles will be revealed!

MERCHANT: A New World means new markets for commerce. I shall grow richer than a duke or king!

FARMER: Amerigo Vespucci saw what Columbus did not see.

SCHOLAR: Too bad Vespucci died a pauper in 1512. His widow, Maria, had to petition the government for a pension.

MERCHANT: But his name will live on! America!

(LIGHTS FADE OUT CENTER; LIGHTS UP RIGHT on Old Spanish John standing at the globe table, with Edward and Elizabeth sitting in their chairs.)

OLD SPANISH JOHN: Over sixty editions of Vespucci's voyage have been printed. Of all the great voyages, his is the most widely published. *(Spins the globe.)* And just seven years ago, mis amigos, the brilliant mapmaker Mercator of Flanders created this object that describes the land mass from the North Pole to the South Pole — as America.

EDWARD: That was quite a ripping yarn, Old John. I suppose it proves my sister's point, right enough.

OLD SPANISH JOHN: Amerigo Vespucci achieved immortality without any effort on his part to become so.

ELIZABETH: I should like to command a ship of discovery when I grow up!

EDWARD: Indeed! That's about as likely as you becoming Queen of England!

OLD SPANISH JOHN: *(Addresses audience.)* Be careful what you wish for, my young friends. "Al fin y al cabo," history has a way of choosing a path for you. *(Spins the globe.)* Even as you sleep, the world never ceases to spin.

(LIGHTS OUT.)

THE END

Everyday Science
in Ben Franklin's America

Benjamin Franklin (1706–90) was an extraordinary man who achieved success as an inventor, scientist, author, publisher, diplomat and co-founder of the United States of America. Born in Boston, he learned the printing trade as a teenager and moved to Philadelphia in 1723, where he quickly became a well-known printer and businessman in this thriving colonial center of commerce and science. Franklin enjoyed commenting on the politics and social customs of his day; under the pen name of "Richard Saunders," or "Poor Richard," he wrote *Poor Richard's Almanack*, a compendium of humorous wit and wisdom that still rings true today over two-and-a-half centuries later.

Franklin's interest in science grew in the 1740s, after he retired from his printing shop. Beginning with the publication of his *Proposal for Promoting Useful Knowledge among the British Plantations in America* in 1743, Franklin explored and attempted to describe in a rigorous scientific manner many natural phenomena, including magnets, clouds, waterspouts, sunspots, earthquakes, and fossils. He is best known for his experiments in electricity and invented what is considered to be the first electrical battery. The experiment in this play is based on an actual experiment Franklin conducted in his early research into the properties of electricity; it is published in his book *Experiments and Observations on Electricity* (1751).

Everyday science in colonial America was very rudimentary and dependent upon information from Europe; scientific research was largely performed by amateurs with little chance to compare their findings to that of other scientists. Franklin urged the scientists of his day to report their discoveries to each other, and he co-founded the American Philosophical Society, the nation's first scientific association. Curiously, Franklin never secured a patent for any of his multitude of inventions. "As we enjoy great advantages from the inventions of others," he wrote, "we should be glad of an opportunity to serve others by an invention of ours, and this we should do freely and generously."

RUNNING TIME: 25 minutes

TIME: 1769

PLACE: Meeting Room of the American Philosophical Society, Philadelphia, Pennsylvania

CAST: 11 actors, min. 3 boys (•), 2 girls (+)
• Benjamin Franklin
+ Mrs. Deborah Franklin
• Chauncy Blatherbite, Visitor from England
+ Paul (Polly) Baker, Servant (age 11)
• Richard Saunders, Scribe (age 11)
   John Ross, Society Member
   Owen Biddle, Society Member
   Dr. Benjamin Rush, Society Member
   Lewis Nicola, Society Member
   Rev. Francis Alison, Society Member
   David Rittenhouse, Society Member

STAGE SET: medium-sized Speaker's Table at mid center; Writing Desk to left of Speaker's Table; an Experiment Table at down right; 2 chairs behind Speaker's Table; 1 chair behind Writing Desk; 2 chairs to left of Writing Desk; 4 chairs to right of Speaker's Table; at opening all characters face audience

PROPS: quill pen, ink pot, parchment paper, gavel, water pitcher, rag, tray of sandwiches, 12-inch glass tube, 2 waxed tile squares (12-inch by 12-inch)

COSTUMES: All characters dress in mid-18th century urban attire — for men: breech-style pants or pants coming to knees with knee-length stockings, ruffled white shirt, dark-colored vest and/or frock-style waist-jacket, buckled shoes; the adult Society members may don a powdered wig or a tri-corner hat; Mrs. Franklin wears a long dress with bunched sleeves at shoulder and an apron; her dress will likely cover her feet, but slippers would suffice for period shoes; Polly Baker is dressed in man's attire with a cap hiding her long hair.

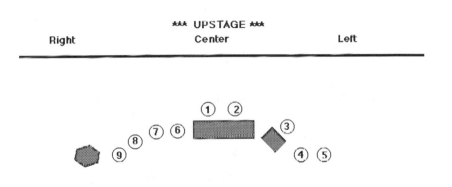

*** UPSTAGE ***

Right   Center   Left

Stage Plan — *Everyday Science in Ben Franklin's America*

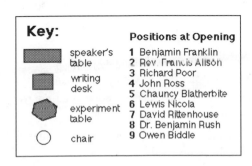

Key:		Positions at Opening
▒	speaker's table	1 Benjamin Franklin
		2 Rev. Francis Allison
▢	writing desk	3 Richard Poor
		4 John Ross
		5 Chauncy Blatherbite
⬡	experiment table	6 Lewis Nicola
		7 David Rittenhouse
		8 Dr. Benjamin Rush
◯	chair	9 Owen Biddle

LIGHTS UP FULL. A group of gentlemen are seated at center stage: BENJAMIN FRANKLIN and REV. FRANCIS ALISON at the Speaker's Table; RICHARD SAUNDERS at the Writing Desk; JOHN ROSS and CHAUNCY BLATHERBITE to left of Writing Desk; DAVID RITTENHOUSE, OWEN BIDDLE, DR. BENJAMIN RUSH and LEWIS NICOLA to right of Speaker's Table. As play opens, Rittenhouse, Biddle, Rush, Nicola, Ross and Blatherbite are speaking among themselves; Richard Saunders, the young Scribe, idly twirls a quill; PAUL BAKER, the young Servant, brings a water pitcher to the Experiment Table; Rev. Francis Alison gavels the meeting to order.

REV. FRANCIS ALISON: The monthly meeting of the American Philosophical Society Held at Philadelphia for Promoting Useful Knowledge will now come to order. Is there any new business?

(John Ross raises his hand.)

JOHN ROSS: Mr. Chairman!
REV. FRANCIS ALISON: Chair recognizes Mr. John Ross.

(John Ross stands.)

JOHN ROSS: Gentlemen. We have today a most distinguished visitor from our mother country. Allow me to introduce Squire Chauncy Blatherbite of London, England.

(Chauncy Blatherbite stands, bows foppishly as Society Members politely applaud.)

JOHN ROSS: Squire Blatherbite is a well-known—
CHAUNCY BLATHERBITE: Oh, you needn't bother! Surely renown of my scientific exploits has preceded me here to the colonies? My reputation as an intellect is unrivalled.
RICHARD SAUNDERS: Indeed, Squire, the man who falls in love with himself will have no rivals.

(Society Members laugh; Chauncy Blatherbite, annoyed, sits down.)

REV. FRANCIS ALISON: Forgive the exuberance of our young scribe, Richard Saunders, and allow me to introduce our present company. I am Reverend Francis Alison, vice-provost of the College of Philadelphia.

JOHN ROSS: *(Stands, bows.)* John Ross, merchant. *(Sits.)*

OWEN BIDDLE: *(Stands, bows.)* Owen Biddle, clockmaker, inventor. *(Sits.)*

DR. BENJAMIN RUSH: *(Stands, bows.)* Dr. Benjamin Rush, physician. *(Sits.)*

DAVID RITTENHOUSE: *(Stands, bows.)* David Rittenhouse, astronomer. *(Sits.)*

LEWIS NICOLA: *(Stands, bows.)* Lewis Nicola, a native of France, s'il vous plait. Bookstore owner and magazine publisher. *(Sits.)*

BENJAMIN FRANKLIN: *(Stands, bows.)* And I am Benjamin Franklin, humble printer and editor of *The Pennsylvania Gazette*

LEWIS NICOLA: Monsieur Franklin is too modest. Why, he is an inventor of the first rank!

OWEN BIDDLE: He invented the Pennsylvania stove and fireplace to better warm our houses.

DR. BENJAMIN RUSH: He invented the lightning rod to protect our houses from catching fire.

DAVID RITTENHOUSE: Don't forget about his three-wheel clock that tells the hour, minute and second.

PAUL BAKER: And the rocking chair, so a working person can relax from toil and contemplate useful thoughts in her leisure time.

(Rev. Alison frowns and look askance at Paul Baker but says nothing.)

JOHN ROSS: Our Dr. Franklin's experiments in natural science have been acclaimed the world over!

LEWIS NICOLA: Monsieur Franklin devised the electrostatic generator.

OWEN BIDDLE: And the electrical air thermometer.

DR. BENJAMIN RUSH: He has analyzed convection in air.

DAVID RITTENHOUSE: And described waterspouts and whirlwinds.

JOHN ROSS: He discovered the Gulf Stream in the ocean.

LEWIS NICOLA: And devised an ocean thermometer for use in navigation.

OWEN BIDDLE: He favors the practice of inoculation against disease.

DR. BENJAMIN RUSH: He suggests electrical shock in the treatment of paralysis.

DAVID RITTENHOUSE: He helped found our first hospital.

LEWIS NICOLA: And our first police force. And circulating library.

RICHARD SAUNDERS: He wrote the first autobiography.

OWEN BIDDLE: Conceived a phonetic alphabet.

PAUL BAKER: And invented the most beautiful musical instrument in the world — the glass harmonica!

(Rev. Alison, Biddle, Rush, Nicola, Rittenhouse, Ross and Blatherbite turn and look askance at Paul Baker, who realizes he has spoken out of turn and lowers head sheepishly.)

PAUL BAKER: Beg pardon, gentlemen. *(Takes out rag and begins wiping Experiment Table.)*

REV. FRANCIS ALISON: I declare, that servant boy has become most vociferous of late.

BENJAMIN FRANKLIN: And filled with much interest in acquiring wisdom.

RICHARD SAUNDERS: It is a fool that cannot conceal his wisdom.

REV. FRANCIS ALISON: Well taken, Richard. But, pray, let us proceed to our main topic. This year of our Lord 1769 will long be remembered in the annals of science. For it is the year of the Transit of Venus!

DAVID RITTENHOUSE: The attention of the entire learned world is directed to this event. And we here in America — all the British colonies, that is — will be afforded the best opportunity to observe this natural phenomenon that will not occur for another one hundred and five years.

OWEN BIDDLE: At last, reliable measurements of the sun's parallax will be possible!

LEWIS NICOLA: Indeed, the powers of Europe are vying to see who will solve the problem! Science has finally become worthy of attention from kings and generals! Our contribution will gain a new respect for American science.

CHAUNCY BLATHERBITE: I wouldn't go that far, old chap. After all, it's just a silly star galloping willy-nilly through the summer sky. If you want to talk about *real* science, let me relate the research I've done on the mystical aura surrounding King George's bottom shoe buckle. It's utterly fascinating and rather—

DR. BENJAMIN RUSH: Pardon me, sir, but are you implying that our American science is of less value because it is practical?

OWEN BIDDLE: In the last few years alone, Americans have invented many useful items. Richard Wells has invented the water-driven ship pump.

LEWIS NICOLA: William Henry has invented a steam-operated register that controls heat.

DR. BENJAMIN RUSH: Dr. Lionel Chalmers of Charleston has published medical essays on the relation of climate and disease.

DAVID RITTENHOUSE: And our own Owen Biddle, modest as he is, has lately invented the file-cutting machine.

JOHN ROSS: *(Stands and claps.)* Huzzah! *(Sits.)*

CHAUNCY BLATHERBITE: You Americans are certainly hog-wild for gadgets!

BENJAMIN FRANKLIN: We must bend science to useful purposes, and apply science to the common concerns of life. Science will make America great and transform this land into one of wealth and freedom.

CHAUNCY BLATHERBITE: All this inventing seems to have given you Americans swelled heads.

RICHARD SAUNDERS: Better to have a swelled head than a shriveled brain.

(All but Chauncy Blatherbite chuckle.)

CHAUNCY BLATHERBITE: *(Stands.)* Very well, then. Show me an example of what you colonials call "science!"

OWEN BIDDLE: *(Stands.)* I accept the challenge!

LEWIS NICOLA: *(Stands.)* I second the acceptance!

REV. FRANCIS ALISON: But first, gentlemen, let us adjourn for lunch.

JOHN ROSS: Where is our lunch?

REV. FRANCIS ALISON: Master Baker has gone to fetch it. Master Baker?

(All eyes turn toward Paul Baker, who has been studying the materials on the Experiment Table.)

REV. FRANCIS ALISON: Master Baker!

(Paul Baker jumps back from table, startled, and begins backing toward right exit.)

PAUL BAKER: I, umm, right away, sirs, yes, beg pardon…

(MRS. DEBORAH FRANKLIN enters from right, carrying a tray of sandwiches; Paul Baker freezes and looks away.)

LEWIS NICOLA: *(Bows.)* Mrs. Franklin!

MRS. DEBORAH FRANKLIN: *(To Paul Baker.)* Polly! I've been looking all over Market Street for you! You left the house this morning with several pots still to scrub!

REV. FRANCIS ALISON: What jest is this?

MRS. DEBORAH FRANKLIN: And what on earth are you doing in that ridiculous attire? Where is your serving dress?

(Mrs. Franklin flips off Paul Baker's hat; a pile of tresses falls out, and Paul is revealed to be a girl; the men — all but Richard Saunders and Benjamin Franklin — gasp and murmur in shock.)

BENJAMIN FRANKLIN: Gentlemen, welcome our kitchen maid, Miss Polly Baker.

JOHN ROSS: A woman in the society hall? This is an outrage!

RICHARD SAUNDERS: Sirs, I am to blame. Polly is my cousin. She prevailed upon me to secret her into this society, and, faith — in all honesty I see no reason why she shouldn't be allowed, though she be a female!

BENJAMIN FRANKLIN: Alas, poor Richard! He has yet to learn that no good deed goes unpunished.

(The members grumble and mutter as Mrs. Franklin takes the sandwich tray around to the members.)

OWEN BIDDLE: But women are ignorant of science!

POLLY BAKER: Being ignorant is no shame, as being unwilling to learn.

BENJAMIN FRANKLIN: Or unwilling to let others learn.

CHAUNCY BLATHERBITE: I disagree entirely. A woman's place is in the home.

(He reaches for a sandwich just as Mrs. Franklin pulls the tray away.)

MRS. DEBORAH FRANKLIN: Then, perhaps you'd best have your lunch at home, sir. *(Exits left.)*

REV. FRANCIS ALISON: I recommend a vote. All in favor of letting Master, er, Miss Baker remain as an obsever to the society, say "Aye!"

ALL EXCEPT CHAUNCY BLATHERBITE: Aye!

(All look at Chauncy Blatherbite, who frowns, pouts, then stamps his foot.)

CHAUNCY BLATHERBITE: Oh, very well — aye!

BENJAMIN FRANKLIN: Excellent! Now, Miss Baker, in lieu of your former employment as a servant boy, we will put you to work as an experimental subject. You will stand on a waxed square, as will Master Saunders.

(Owen Biddle and Dr. Benjamin Rush place waxed tile squares on floor at down center. David Rittenhouse directs Polly Baker to stand on the rightmost square facing the audience, Richard Saunders on the other,

also facing the audience. Benjamin Franklin takes glass tube from Experiment Table and holds it aloft.)

BENJAMIN FRANKLIN: This glass experiment tube was given to me by the English scientist Peter Collinson, when helping me start my first research into electricity. He passed on from this mortal coil last year, and I dedicate this experiment to his memory.

CHAUNCY BLATHERBITE: We may *all* pass on before Dr. Franklin readies his experiment.

BENJAMIN FRANKLIN: Indeed, we require one more subject. Squire Blatherbite, if you please?

CHAUNCY BLATHERBITE: Moi? Oh, very well. I simply adore charades! What shall I be?

BENJAMIN FRANKLIN: You, Squire, shall be the "uninsulated" subject.

(Chauncy Blatherbite stands to the left of Richard Saunders and faces the audience.)

BENJAMIN FRANKLIN: I draw the society's attention to the jar on the table. It is a "Leyden jar," a form of condenser, or capacitor, named after the European city where it was discovered. Now, when the Leyden jar is grounded and an electrical charge introduced into the water, the two states of Electricity — the plus and minus — are combined and balanced in this miraculous container.

CHAUNCY BLATHERBITE: States of Electricity! Why, it sounds rather like a geography lesson!

(Benjamin Franklin gives glass tube to Polly Baker.)

BENJAMIN FRANKLIN: Miss Baker holds the glass tube. Rub your hands up and down the length a few times, Polly. Now, Richard, draw your hand near the tube, but without touching it. Stay on your squares, mind you!

JOHN ROSS: A spark jumps to his hand!

BENJAMIN FRANKLIN: Now, Richard, turn and face the Squire. And give him a good old-fashioned Yankee Doodle welcome!

(Richard Saunders shakes hands with Chauncy Blatherbite, who receives a slight electrical shock and leaps in the air, yelping and holding his hand in pain.)

CHAUNCY BLATHERBITE: Yiiiii! I'm on fire!

(Blatherbite runs to the water pitcher and sticks in his hand, as the others laugh.)

BENJAMIN FRANKLIN: The experiment is a success! Squire Blatherbite has become a "charged" subject! Can anyone tell how this experiment worked?

LEWIS NICOLA: At the beginning, each of the subjects possess an equal amount of natural electricity.

DR. BENJAMIN RUSH: When Miss Baker rubbed the tube, she transferred *her* electricity to the tube.

POLLY BAKER: When Richard put his hand near the tube, he was gathering *my* electricity.

DR. BENJAMIN RUSH: And becoming a charged subject.

REV. FRANCIS ALISON: Yet Polly and Richard were protected from shock by standing on the waxed squares.

OWEN BIDDLE: And when the Squire shook hands with young Richard—

DAVID RITTENHOUSE: All the electricity jumped to him!

RICHARD SAUNDERS: Three cheers for American electricity!

NICOLA, SAUNDERS, RUSH, ALISON, BIDDLE & RITTENHOUSE: Hip-hip-hooray! Hip-hip-hooray! Hip-hip-hooray!

(Benjamin Franklin turns to Chauncy Blatherbite.)

BENJAMIN FRANKLIN: And why, I wonder, did the electricity *not* diminish on its indirect route to Squire Blatherbite? Surely, mere wax cannot withstand the element of electrical fire?

CHAUNCY BLATHERBITE: Because the electrical charge never lessened, but passed through each conducting body, continuing to circulate...and *build*, blast it!

(The company chuckles.)

BENJAMIN FRANKLIN: Excellent, good Squire. The chief lesson we have learnt, gentlemen — and milady — is that electrical effects do not result merely from man's manipulations, but are part of nature itself…the very essential routines of nature.

CHAUNCY BLATHERBITE: I congratulate you, Dr. Franklin. But how could you be so certain the experiment would turn out as you predicted?

BENJAMIN FRANKLIN: Well, I—

RICHARD SAUNDERS: When a man is absolutely certain, doubt smiles.

BENJAMIN FRANKLIN: Quite right, Richard. I must take note of some of these proverbs you quote.

RICHARD SAUNDERS: I keep a list of them, sir. Right here in this almanack. *(Holds up parchment.)*

BENJAMIN FRANKLIN: Good lad. Mr. Chairman!

REV. FRANCIS ALISON: Yes, Dr. Franklin?

BENJAMIN FRANKLIN: I suggest we briefly adjourn and make room for our Junior Society members. *(Peers into audience.)* I see them gathering in the courtyard. Perhaps they would like to help us with some additional experiments?

CHAUNCY BLATHERBITE: Let that rabble in our hallow chambers?

POLLY BAKER: And why not, sir? After all, in America, the doors of wisdom are never shut!

(LIGHTS OUT.)

THE END

"Lady of the Lamp":
Florence Nightingale, Founder of Modern Nursing

Florence Nightingale (1820–1910) was raised in a wealthy home in England and was destined by her upbringing to grow up to be nothing more than a society party-giver. At age seventeen, however, she had a dream in which she heard a voice call her to serve others. Seven years later, she decided to become a nurse, even though at the time nurses were considered little better than unskilled servants and hospitals were a place people went to die without hope of getting better. Florence persevered in her nursing studies, and when the Crimean War broke out in 1854, she was called upon by the British government to organize a regiment of nurses to assist in the battlefield hospitals. Florence's innovations in how to treat patients revolutionized hospital care and led to many reforms in the practice of medicine. Today's hospitals, with their bright and cheery hallways and recreation rooms, flowers, nutritious food and well-trained nurses, are a direct result of her inspiration and compassion. In 1907, three years before her death, she received the Order of Merit from King Edward VII of England — the first time this lofty honor was ever bestowed upon a woman.

RUNNING TIME: 20 minutes

TIME: 1884; 1854–55

PLACE: Nightingale Training School for Nurses, London, England; Barrack Hospital, Scutari, Turkey

CAST: 12 actors, min. 6 boys (•), 6 girls (+)

+ Florence Nightingale
+ Headmistress Logan
+ Nurse Logan
+ Nurse Sinclair
+ Harriet Embley, Nursing Student
+ Hilary Hurst, Nursing Student

• Alexis Soyer
• Dr. John Hall
• Lord Stratford Canning
• McAllister, Wounded Soldier
• Rhys, Wounded Soldier
• O'Hara, Wounded Soldier

STAGE SET: three hospital pallets on floor at mid center; small table and chair at down left

PROPS: scrub brush, water bucket, broom, ornate walking cane, soup pot, 2 spice jars, paper hand fan, towel, water bowl, quill, piece of writing paper, Turkish lamp (a single candle inside a round collapsible paper shade)

COSTUMES: Florence Nightingale wears a long Victorian-style grey house dress, white apron, white lace collar and white bonnet; Nurse Logan and Nurse Sinclair wear the same uniform as Florence Nightingale but without lace collar; Harriet Embley and Hilary Hurst wear the same uniform but their caps are more like traditional modern nurse caps; Headmistress Logan wears a long grey dress without apron, collar or bonnet; Wounded Soldiers have patches of mid-19th-century military uniforms and are swathed in bandages; Dr. John Hall wears a British officer's outfit; Lord Stratford Canning wears a period upper-class gentleman's suit; Alexis Soyer also wears a period gentleman's suit along with a white kitchen apron

Stage Plan —"Lady of the Lamp": Florence Nightingale, Founder of Modern Nursing

Key: table   chair   pallet

LIGHTS UP RIGHT on HILARY HURST and HARRIET EMBLEY at down right. Hilary is on her knees scrubbing the floor, while Harriet stands, fussing with the bristles of her broom and avoiding real work.

HILARY HURST: Oh, my poor knees! Harriet! Are you going to do a lick of work at all?

HARRIET EMBLEY: In my household, Hilary dear, they had servants to perform this sort of common labor. This is England, after all!

HILARY HURST: Well, I did plenty of work around *my* house. But here at school — I cannot fathom why we're treated like workhouse inmates instead of nursing students!

HEADMISTRESS LOGAN: *(O.S. up right.)* Are you going to dance with that broom, or sweep with it, Miss Embley?

(SPOTLIGHT UP RIGHT on HEADMISTRESS LOGAN standing up right, arms folded, frowning.)

HILARY HURST: Headmistress Logan! *(Scrubs furiously.)*

HARRIET EMBLEY: Good morning, madam. So good to see you. Miss Hurst had a question for you regarding our curriculum.

(Headmistress Logan strides forward and stands directly in front of Hilary Hurst, who rises and stands nervously.)

HILARY HURST: Well, that is, I, um—

HEADMISTRESS LOGAN: You may speak freely.

HILARY HURST: Thank you, ma'am. *(Clears throat.)* We've all learned a lot here at Nightingale Training School for Nurses. How to tend the sick.

HARRIET EMBLEY: How to dress wounds.

HILARY HURST: How to assist in childbirth.

HARRIET EMBLEY: How to administer anaesthetics.

HILARY HURST: But, Nurse Logan, what does scrubbing the chips off an old wood floor have to do with being a nurse?

HARRIET EMBLEY: We're here to treat ailing people not cobwebbed ceilings!

HEADMISTRESS LOGAN: *(Chuckles.)* Girls, girls, girls. Oh, if Miss Nightingale could hear you talk! *(Grabs broom out of Harriet Embley's hands, brandishes it fiercely.)* She'd give you the sack quicker than you could say streptococcus!

HILARY HURST: Streptococcus — the oval-shaped bacteria that causes strep throat and other deadly respiratory infections!

HEADMISTRESS LOGAN: Indeed! You *are* learning something! Then learn this: your job as nurses will be to fight disease wherever you find it. And right now, it lives in every flake of dirt inhabiting this room. Why, when Miss Nightingale and her nurses landed at Barrack Hospital in Scutari, the first thing she had us do was scrub floors!

HARRIET EMBLEY: You were there? With Florence Nightingale in Turkey?

HEADMISTRESS LOGAN: We arrived on November 3, 1854, thirty years ago almost to this very day. England was fighting Russia in the Crimean War, and the battlefield hospitals were overwhelmed. A call went out for nurses, and Florence assembled thirty-eight volunteers. It was the first time women had been employed by the British Army to nurse the wounded.

(LIGHTS OUT RIGHT; LIGHTS UP LEFT on FLORENCE NIGHTINGALE standing at down left, with NURSE LOGAN and NURSE SINCLAIR standing behind her; Florence Nightingale surveys the scene, looking across stage. SOUND: Groans from WOUNDED SOLDIERS lying on pallets at mid-center stage.)

NURSE LOGAN: Miss Nightingale, ma'am, if you beg my saying so, but this is bloody awful!

NURSE SINCLAIR: Four miles of beds, if you can call them that, each one not eighteen inches apart. Twenty-three hundred wounded men lying in blood and filth!

NURSE LOGAN: No furniture, no food, no cooking utensils, blankets, lamps, candles or supplies of any kind!

NURSE SINCLAIR: Not even a cup to bring a dying man a last drink of water!

NURSE LOGAN: I've yet to see a doctor anywhere!

NURSE SINCLAIR: Vermin crawling everywhere! *(Jumps, pulls her skirt away from floor, points right.)* Eeek! That rat was big as a terrier!

NURSE LOGAN: Oh, Miss Nightingale, ma'am, what are we going to do?

FLORENCE NIGHTINGALE: I can truly say like St. Peter that "it is good for us to be here." Though I doubt whether St. Peter were here, *he* would say so!

(LIGHTS UP CENTER as DR. JOHN HALL, carrying an ornate walking cane, enters from right, strides across stage and meets Florence Nightingale and Nurse Logan and Nurse Sinclair at down center.)

DR. JOHN HALL: Ladies! I am Dr. John Hall, Chief of Medical Staff of the British Expeditionary Army. *(Bows stiffly.)* I trust you've found your quarters comfortable.

FLORENCE NIGHTINGALE: *(Curtsies stiffly.)* I found the rotting corpse of a Russian general in my room. He was beyond the ken of comfort.

DR. JOHN HALL: Right you are! Carry on! *(Points with cane to men lying in cots.)* We'll have one of these slugabeds distribute the books. Lazy brutes, not a one able to read, I wager. *(Turns to exit right.)*

FLORENCE NIGHTINGALE: Dr. Hall! When do we begin treating the wounded?

DR. JOHN HALL: *(Turns back to face her.)* I beg your pardon?

FLORENCE NIGHTINGALE: We're the nurses you requested. We've come to treat the wounded.

DR. JOHN HALL: Nurses? Good heavens, I thought you were the Ladies from the Library League!

FLORENCE NIGHTINGALE: If you can take us to the operating room, we will assist the doctors—

DR. JOHN HALL: Absolutely not! Nurses are forbidden to assist doctors! Nurses are forbidden to attend the wounded! What do you think this is, madam?

FLORENCE NIGHTINGALE: A hospital filled with sick and dying soldiers who, having bravely served their Queen and country, deserve the best medical treatment the army can offer.

DR. JOHN HALL: Scum of the earth, and nothing more! *(Raps one of the pallets with cane.)* Don't spoil them with unnecessary kindness!

FLORENCE NIGHTINGALE: Dr. Hall!

DR. JOHN HALL: Right you are! Carry on! *(Turns, marches offstage right.)*

FLORENCE NIGHTINGALE: *(Turns to Nurse Logan and Nurse Sinclair.)* Very well, nurses. You've heard the commanding officer. Let's get to work. Nurse Logan, organize a cleaning detail. Every inch of this hospital will be scrubbed clean until every flea, every maggot, every rat has fled into the Black Sea!

NURSE LOGAN: Yes, ma'am. *(Exits left.)*

FLORENCE NIGHTINGALE: Nurse Sinclair, start making decent bedding and bandages. Pillows, too, and warm shirts. Winter's coming on, and those who have survived cholera and dysentery will be soon facing pneumonia.

NURSE SINCLAIR: Yes, ma'am. And where will you be working?

FLORENCE NIGHTINGALE: In the kitchen. If it's true an army lives on its stomach, *this* army isn't going to live very long at all!

(Nurse Sinclair exits left; Florence Nightingale crosses to table at mid left and, from behind the table, she pulls up a large soup pot and two spice jars and begins measuring from jars into pot.)

MCALLISTER: Miss Nightingale discovered the hospital food was killing the men instead of helping them.

O'HARA: But she had brought her own healthy food supplies, even portable stoves to cook them in!

RHYS: She introduced a new diet that helped the wounded regain their strength. Men who previously would have died because of unsanitary conditions and rancid food were now recovering quite nicely.

MCALLISTER: After the doctors saw the improving conditions, they relented and allowed the nurses to tend the wounded.

O'HARA: Within a few weeks, the mortality rate in the hospital had fallen from forty percent to just two per cent. From forty men out of a hundred to just two!

RHYS: All due to Miss Nightingale's skill at making order out of chaos.

(ALEXIS SOYER enters from left and addresses Florence Nightingale.)

ALEXIS SOYER: *(Bows deeply.)* Mademoiselle Nightingale, je m'appelle Alexis Soyer!

FLORENCE NIGHTINGALE: The famous chef from Paris!

ALEXIS SOYER: But of course!

FLORENCE NIGHTINGALE: You organized soup kitchens in Dublin during the Irish Famine and saved thousands of people from starvation.

ALEXIS SOYER: Ah, yes, I taught the society ladies how to make potato soup! They so loved being useful!

FLORENCE NIGHTINGALE: Chef Soyer, we desperately need your skills here. The Battle of Inkerman has sent thousands of casualties to our hospital, and we have no means to feed them.

ALEXIS SOYER: But you are in luck, mademoiselle. I have brought a team of trained chefs. We will build new ovens and create a bakery for fresh bread. We will create nutritious menus from these boring army rations. We will train your orderlies how to properly prepare food. And, yes, we will even make cooks out of Englishmen! *(Exits left.)*

(LORD STRATFORD CANNING, carrying a paper hand fan, enters from right and strolls across stage to down center.)

LORD STRATFORD CANNING: So this is the Barrack Hospital. Quite cheery!

FLORENCE NIGHTINGALE: Lord Stratford Canning, the British Ambassador!

LORD STRATFORD CANNING: *(Peers down at McAllister.)* My goodness, that's a nasty bruise.

MCALLISTER: They amputated my left leg, sir.

LORD STRATFORD CANNING: Jolly good!

FLORENCE NIGHTINGALE: Lord Canning, I must speak to you!

(Florence Nightingale crosses briskly to down center.)

LORD STRATFORD CANNING: Oh, yes, Miss Hightindale.

FLORENCE NIGHTINGALE: Nightingale. Florence Nightingale.

LORD STRATFORD CANNING: Jolly good!

FLORENCE NIGHTINGALE: Lord Canning, you promised two months ago to repair the hospital wing damaged by fire. Each new battle brings in hundreds of casualties. We must have the space to treat them!

LORD STRATFORD CANNING: There's been a problem with the workmen we've hired. It seems they don't know how to actually *do* repairs.

FLORENCE NIGHTINGALE: Then fire them and hire new ones!

LORD STRATFORD CANNING: My dear Miss Bightinbale, it's much more complicated. You see, these are Turkish workmen provided by the Grand Pasha of Constantinople. He would be highly offended if we were to tell him his workmen were unqualified. He might just jolly well lop off their heads! *(Makes throat-cutting gesture with fan.)* Ha-ha-ha!

FLORENCE NIGHTINGALE: Three of every four British soliders in this war are under medical treatment. Half of those are dying — not from the wounds they got in battle, but from the diseases they contract at this hospital! There is open sewage flowing through the west ward!

LORD STRATFORD CANNING: *(Sniffs the air.)* I thought I detected an odor!

FLORENCE NIGHTINGALE: Very well. If you will not end this crisis, I shall. I am hiring two hundred new workers to repair the hospital.

LORD STRATFORD CANNING: And with whose money?

FLORENCE NIGHTINGALE: With *my* money! You may put a cost on the lives of these soldiers, Lord Canning, but I will spend every last cent I possess to see them convalesce in comfort and dignity.

LORD STRATFORD CANNING: You are impertinent!

(Lord Stratford Canning stalks off to exit right, turning every few feet to splutter at Florence Nightingale; Florence Nightingale crosses to table and picks up a lamp; Nurse Logan and Nurse Sinclair enter from left, Nurse Logan carrying a towel, Nurse Sinclair a bowl of water.)

LORD STRATFORD CANNING: You are disrespectful to authority! You are so, so — jolly good! *(Exits right.)*

(Florence Nightingale goes to Wounded Soldiers and helps adjust their pillows and bandages, followed by Nurse Logan and Nurse Sinclair who also tend the men.)

MCALLISTER: Florence got her new workmen, and the building was repaired.

O'HARA: Donations to her cause poured in from England — many of them from common working people giving whatever little they had to help those less fortunate.

RHYS: No matter what the hour, Florence was always on the job.

MCALLISTER: She stood next to the men as they endured terrible surgery.

O'HARA: What a comfort it was to see her pass on her daily rounds through the hospital! She spoke to each patient personally.

RHYS: If she couldn't see everyone during the day, she returned at night.

MCALLISTER: Four miles of beds, she visited each one, a large Turkish lamp lighting her way.

O'HARA: We would kiss her shadow as it fell against the wall, and lay back on our pillow, content.

RHYS: She gave us respect.

MCALLISTER: She gave us hope.

O'HARA: The men even stopped using foul language for the sake of the Lady with the Lamp.

RHYS: Bloody right!

FLORENCE NIGHTINGALE: *(To audience.)* The tears come into my eyes as I think how, amidst scenes of loathsome disease and death, there rose above it all the innate dignity, gentleness and chivalry of the men…shining in what must be considered the lowest sinks of human misery. They are the true heroes of this campaign. And the nurses! One hundred and eight nurses served in the Crimea. Sixty-four were sent home ill. Six died. It is impossible to estimate too highly the unwearied devotion, patience and cheerfulness, the judgment and activity and the single-heartedness with which these women have labored in the service of the sick.

(Florence Nightingale crosses to table, sets down lamp and takes up quill and paper to write; Nurse Logan and Nurse Sinclair stand behind Wounded Soldiers.)

NURSE LOGAN: Florence Nightingale was among the first in the medical field to realize the importance of cleanliness and proper diet in helping the sick get better.

NURSE SINCLAIR: Even before bacteria and viruses were discovered, she argued that taking steps to prevent disease was as important as what was done to cure it.

NURSE LOGAN: And she didn't confine her reforms to the hospital bedside. She studied how hospitals were built and maintained.

NURSE SINCLAIR: She suggested more windows and better ventilation.

MCALLISTER: Improved drainage.

O'HARA: Less crowded conditions.

RHYS: Hospitals all over the world sought her advice.

NURSE LOGAN: But her greatest contribution to human healing was the establishment of standards for nursing.

NURSE SINCLAIR: In 1859 she wrote a book, *"Notes on Nursing: What It Is, and What It Is Not."* It was the first textbook that defined the training of nurses.

NURSE LOGAN: The following year, she established the Nightingale Training School for Nurses at St. Thomas Hospital in London.

FLORENCE NIGHTINGALE: *(Writing.)* Each student will receive her own uniforms, books, room and board. They shall have flowers, pictures and maps to make their studies more pleasant and their minds more open to acquiring knowledge. Those successful in the year-long course will be placed on the hospital register as Certified Nurses.

(LIGHTS FADE DOWN CENTER; LIGHTS FADE UP RIGHT.)

HEADMISTRESS LOGAN: In the quarter century since, the graduates of this nursing school have served with distinction at hospitals in every corner of the globe.

HILARY HURST: *(Sighs.)* And they've all started out scrubbing floors.

HARRIET EMBLEY: *(Takes broom from Headmistress Logan.)* And sweeping cobwebs.

HEADMISTRESS LOGAN: Indeed! So they can start saving lives.

FLORENCE NIGHTINGALE: *(To audience.)* The woman who life chooses to be a nurse must feel it a privilege — not a sacrifice — to attend the sick. I ask only that my people will think to themselves and say to others: "At least she did deliberately what she thought right."

(LIGHTS OUT.)

THE END

Edward Jenner
and the Gossip of Milkmaids

Throughout the 1600s and 1700s, diseases like smallpox, cholera, measles, typhus and various forms of plague raged unabated throughout the world, causing hundreds of thousands of deaths. These diseases afflicted the rich as well as poor — Queen Mary II of England succumbed to smallpox in 1694. Edward Jenner (1749–1823) was an English country physician who established the initial concepts of *preventive medicine*. By meticulously studying the development of cowpox — a less virulent form of smallpox — he was able to discover the process of *vaccination* to ward off disease. This led to improved methods of public health that have made our world a safer place to live. Today, at the close of the 20th century, there are no known cases of smallpox in human beings anywhere in the world.

RUNNING TIME: 20 minutes

TIME: 1766–1796

PLACE: Village of Berkeley, Gloucester, England

CAST: 10 actors, min. 6 boys (•), 3 girls (+)
- • Edward Jenner (teenager)
- • Dr. Ludlow
- • Edward Gardner
- + Farmwife
- • James Phipps (age 8)
- • Edward Jenner (grownup)
- + Milkmaid
- • Roddy Kite
- + Sarah Nelmes, milkmaid
-   Narrator

STAGE SET: at down left a table and a stool on either side; on the table at opening are 2 glass medicine bottles, lotion swab in a swab cup, a notebook, inkpot and quill pen; at mid-center are 2 cows

PROPS: 2 glass medicine bottles, lotion swab, swab cup, cloth bandages, notebook, parchment paper, quill pen, inkpot, bucket, handful of hay, hand magnifying glass, newspaper

COSTUMES: All characters dress in late-18th century country attire — for men: breech-style pants or pants coming to knees with knee-length stockings, ruffled white shirt, dark-colored vest and/or frock-style waist-jacket, buckled shoes; Dr. Ludlow may don a powdered wig; Milkmaid, Sarah Nelmes and Farmwife wear a long plain pleated dress with a wide waist sash; the dress will likely cover their feet, but slippers would suffice for period shoes; Milkmaid and Sarah Nelmes each wear a wide-brim straw bonnet with bright red or blue ties strings; Farmwife can wear an apron.

4

Stage Plan — *Edward Jenner and the Gossip of Milkmaids*

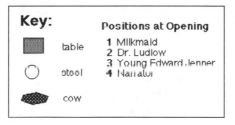

Key:
Positions at Opening

□ table
1 Milkmaid
2 Dr. Ludlow
3 Young Edward Jenner
○ stool
4 Narrator

cow

LIGHTS UP RIGHT on NARRATOR standing at down right, addressing audience.

NARRATOR: Throughout the eighteenth century, the smallpox virus raged unabated around the world. Hundreds of thousands of people suffered disfigurement and, in most cases, death from this cruel plague. Yet, even as the epidemic raged, the seeds of its eventual defeat were being sown in the English countryside.

(LIGHTS OUT ON NARRATOR; LIGHTS UP LEFT on DR. LUDLOW standing at table at down left; A MILKMAID sits on the stool, holding her right arm flat on the table and down, with the index finger extended; YOUNG EDWARD JENNER stands to the left of the table and holds a swath of bandages. Dr. Ludlow daubs the Milkmaid's finger with a swab.)

DR. LUDLOW: This sore on your finger is only a mild case of cowpox, my dear. You are a very lucky young girl.
MILKMAID: Thank you, Dr. Ludlow.
DR. LUDLOW: Very lucky, indeed. Isn't she, Edward?
YOUNG EDWARD JENNER: Yes, sir. She is quite well-favored.

(Instead of listening to Dr. Ludlow, the Milkmaid looks over at Young Edward Jenner and smiles at him, adjusts her bonnet, fingers her scarf, while Dr. Ludlow ties a bandage on her finger.)

DR. LUDLOW: Here we are in modern times, the year 1766! And we're less healthy than our grandparents were. Disease everywhere! Twenty more dead in the village from smallpox last week alone!
MILKMAID: *(Still smiling at Young Edward Jenner.)* Thank you, Dr. Ludlow.
DR. LUDLOW: You never know who might be next. Why, it could be you, dearie. And then that pretty, fresh face of yours wouldn't look so lovely all pocked and pitted!
MILKMAID: *(Turning to Dr. Ludlow.)* Smallpox? Why, doctor, I cannot take that illness!

YOUNG EDWARD JENNER: And, pray, miss, why not?

MILKMAID: *(Displays her bandaged finger.)* Because I have had the cowpox!

DR. LUDLOW: *(Laughs.)* Oh, that is rich! Do you hear that, my young apprentice?

YOUNG EDWARD JENNER: Hear what, sir?

DR. LUDLOW: This delightful village healing lore. These simple country girls actually believe a dose of cowpox will keep them safe from smallpox. *(Laughs.)*

MILKMAID: It will! My four sisters all swear it! And they've been milkmaids near a score of years!

DR. LUDLOW: Indeed, my dear, I'm sure they do so swear. Remember, Edward Jenner, whenever you visit your patients, don't forget to take a cow with you.

(LIGHTS OUT LEFT; Dr. Ludlow, Milkmaid and Young Edward Jenner exit left; LIGHTS UP RIGHT on NARRATOR standing at down right, addressing audience.)

NARRATOR: Edward Jenner went on to medical school in London. After graduating, he returned to his home village of Berkeley to practice general medicine. Though he had absorbed much scientific knowledge over the years, he had never forgotten that longago afternoon with the milkmaid and Dr. Ludlow.

(LIGHTS OUT ON NARRATOR; LIGHTS UP LEFT on ADULT EDWARD JENNER sitting on stool at table at down left; he writes in the notebook and gazes into the audience with a pensive air.)

EDWARD JENNER: "I cannot take that illness"…hmmm…

(SOUND OFFSTAGE LEFT: a knock at the door startles Edward Jenner from his reverie. EDWARD GARDNER, with a slight limp, enters from left, followed by RODDY KITE.)

RODDY KITE: What ho! The country doctor at repose!

EDWARD JENNER: *(Stands, shakes Kite's hand.)* Roddy Kite! I haven't seen you since university!

RODDY KITE: I imagined you'd be out delivering a flock of farmer's babies this fine morn!

EDWARD GARDNER: Not a chance! Too busy treating gout-ridden poets like me. And contemplating the mysteries of the medical universe.

(Edward Gardner sits gingerly on stool; Roddy Kite stands to his left.)

RODDY KITE: He does have that faraway look in his eyes, doesn't he, Gardner? What is it this time, Edward — a cure for cross eyes? A pill to prevent bow legs? *(Laughs.)*

EDWARD JENNER: No, gentlemen. In fact, just as you entered, I was thinking about…smallpox.

RODDY KITE: Nasty illness, that. Going around quite strong just south of here, I've heard.

EDWARD GARDNER: Jenner has a theory about smallpox.

RODDY KITE: Oh?

EDWARD JENNER: I believe there is one type of cowpox that gives protection against smallpox.

RODDY KITE: Not that same old rubbish about cows and their bloody pox?

EDWARD GARDNER: Hear him out, Roddy!

RODDY KITE: A farmer's boy in Newport died of smallpox a fortnight ago, after a terrible case of cowpox the month before. How can you explain that?

EDWARD JENNER: Many cow diseases produce running sores on the hands of their human milkers, and they are all called by the name of cowpox. But not all these sores *are* cowpox. My theory is that only the *true* cowpox disease can prevent smallpox.

RODDY KITE: Good heavens, man! Have you taken leave of your senses? A doctor should not be constructing scientific theory from the gossip of milkmaids! Take a journey down to Newport, if you like. You'll see poxy cows to last from here to next Sunday!

(LIGHTS OUT LEFT; Edward Gardner and Roddy Kite exit left, while Edward Jenner crosses to mid center; LIGHTS UP RIGHT on NARRATOR standing at down right, addressing audience.)

NARRATOR: Edward Jenner took his friend's advice and made the trip to Newport, which was in the midst of a horrifying smallpox epidemic.

(LIGHTS OUT ON NARRATOR; LIGHTS UP CENTER on Edward Jenner at mid center, using a hand magnifying glass to examine the heads and bodies of the two cows standing there; A FARMWIFE, carrying a bucket of hay, enters from right and crosses to center to feed the cows.)

EDWARD JENNER: I say there, madam. Do any of your milkmaids have the cowpox?
FARMWIFE: Indeed, sir, they do. And like you said, it's what you called the "true cowpox."
EDWARD JENNER: I see. And some have contracted smallpox?
FARMWIFE: They have, sir. All of them.
EDWARD JENNER: Would you tell me where I can see them?
FARMWIFE: Why, you can see them from here, sir. *(Points to audience.)* They reside yonder — in the cemetery.

(Farmwife ambles off right, exiting, while Edward Jenner continues to examine the cows; Edward Gardner enters from left and crosses to mid center.)

EDWARD GARDNER: Ah, the poetry to be found in a Gloucester barnyard!
EDWARD JENNER: And the knowledge to be found in a Gloucester cow. Gardner, examine the sore on this animal.

(Edward Jenner hands the magnifying glass to Edward Gardner, who peers at the head of the first cow.)

EDWARD JENNER: Now the sore on its mate.

(Edward Gardner peers at the flank of the second cow.)

EDWARD JENNER: I'll save you the suspense. The disease is the same, true cowpox. But the stages of the disease appear to be different.

EDWARD GARDNER: An astute observation, doctor. And your hypothesis?

EDWARD JENNER: What if at each stage of the disease, the infectious matter in the sore were different?

EDWARD GARDNER: And that at a certain stage—

EDWARD JENNER: The cowpox could still cause sores on the hands of a milkmaid—

EDWARD GARDNER: But not protect against smallpox!

EDWARD JENNER: It is only a theory, mind.

EDWARD GARDNER: But brilliant, nonetheless! How will you test it?

EDWARD JENNER: *(Sighs.)* That, my friend, I do not know.

(LIGHTS OUT CENTER; Edward Gardner exits right, while Edward Jenner crosses to down left; LIGHTS UP RIGHT on NARRATOR standing at down right, addressing audience; LIGHTS UP LEFT on Edward Jenner, pacing to and fro behind the table.)

NARRATOR: During the next nine years, Jenner studied hundreds of cows and their milkers. One bright spring day in May, 1796, Sarah Nelmes — a local milkmaid — was brought into his office. She was suffering with a bad case of cowpox.

(LIGHTS OUT ON NARRATOR; SARAH NELMES sits on stool, holding her bare right arm flat on the table and down as Edward Jenner examines the sores on the arm.)

SARAH NELMES: I can hardly do my milking chores, Dr. Jenner. It itches something terrible.

EDWARD JENNER: I don't doubt that, Sarah. I'd say the disease is at its peak.

SARAH NELMES: You've seen it this bad before?

EDWARD JENNER: Yes. But never in my office. Sarah, I wonder if—

(SOUND OFFSTAGE RIGHT: children shouting at play outside the office. Edward Jenner moves a few steps to right, peering toward down right.)

SARAH NELMES: Children at play. Wonderful to be innocent like that.

EDWARD JENNER: The caretaker's brood. Healthy-looking fellows. *(Looks up to ceiling.)*

MILKMAID: *(O.S.)* Why, doctor, I cannot take that illness!

EDWARD JENNER: *(Calls to right.)* James! James, will you come here a moment, please?

(JAMES PHIPPS enters from right, skipping to meet Edward Jenner, who takes the boy by the hand and leads him to the table and sits him on the second stool.)

EDWARD JENNER: James, are you a brave boy?

JAMES PHIPPS: Why, I don't know, sir. I believe I might be. I want to be a soldier someday and fight old Napoleon!

EDWARD JENNER: Well then, I think you *are* brave enough for this experiment. Have you ever been inoculated?

JAMES PHIPPS: No, sir. But I've heard tell they do it in London and such faraway places.

EDWARD JENNER: If you're brave enough, we're going to try it here.

JAMES PHIPPS: I am, sir! Ask anyone! Ask that milkmaid, if you like!

EDWARD JENNER: That's a good lad! Now, let's hope I'm as brave as you.

(LIGHTS UP RIGHT on NARRATOR standing at down right, addressing audience, as Edward Jenner uses swab to transfer matter from Sarah's sore into the arm of James Phipps.)

NARRATOR: On that day, Edward Jenner performed the first vaccination in the history of medicine. Two months later, after inoculating the boy with infectious matter from a smallpox victim, Jenner wrote to his friend Gardner:

(James Phipps and Sarah Nelmes freeze in place as Edward Gardner, carrying parchment letter, enters from right as Edward Jenner writes in notebook.)

EDWARD JENNER: I have at length accomplished what I have been so long waiting for — the passing of the vaccine virus from one human being to another by the ordinary mode of inoculation. A boy by the name of Phipps was inoculated in the arm from a pustule on the hand of a young woman infected by her master's cows.

EDWARD GARDNER: *(Reading letter.)* The boy has since been inoculated for the smallpox, which, as I ventured to predict, produced no effects. I shall now pursue my experiments with redoubled ardor.

(Roddy Kite, grasping a newspaper, rushes in from left.)

RODDY KITE: *(Reading newspaper.)* "The Times has recently learned of a historic scientific paper by the physician Edward Jenner — *An Inquiry into the Causes and Effects of the Variolae Vaccinae* — that describes his program of inoculating children with a vaccine made from cowpox, the word 'vaccine' deriving from the Latin word for cow." *(Shuts paper and addresses audience.)* Good heavens, I hope the children haven't begun to moo!

NARRATOR: Mail from around the world poured in requesting news of Jenner's technique!

JAMES PHIPPS: Vaccination was taken up in France and Germany!

SARAH NELMES: Spain and Austria!

EDWARD GARDNER: Greece, Turkey and the Middle East!

JAMES PHIPPS: South America and the Caribbean!

SARAH NELMES: China and India!

RODDY KITE: *(Reading newspaper.)* Why, the President of the United

States, Thomas Jefferson, has himself received a vaccination. Bloody good, Prezzie! Bloody good!

(Edward Jenner steps to down center; SPOTLIGHT on Edward Jenner, as OTHER LIGHTS DIM TO HALF.)

NARRATOR: Yet, in England, Edward Jenner did not receive the recognition his discovery deserved. The medical establishment of his day regarded him with jealousy and considered him no more than a simple country doctor, despite the fact that by Jenner's death in 1823, the scourge of smallpox had largely vanished from the face of the earth — and from the faces of human beings.

EDWARD JENNER: *(To audience.)* Someday the practice of vaccination will spread over the entire world. When that day comes, smallpox and other diseases will be no more.

NARRATOR: Edward Jenner succeeded in changing the course of human history by listening to the wisdom of the common people…and by *not* listening to those whose minds were closed by doubt and fear.

(LIGHTS OUT.)

THE END

Anthropology, the Science of Us

Though the science of anthropology has achieved its greatest advances in the 20th century, it is rooted in the explorations and discoveries of the longago past. Anthropology studies the "human animal" and the incredibly complex collection of ideas, practices, rituals, behavior patterns and activities that make up human culture, from how we organize our families and schools to how we display emotion at sports events and funerals. The anthropologist is an explorer who seeks to discover what lies in the uncharted depths of the ocean of human experience.

RUNNING TIME: 20 minutes

TIME: Right now

PLACE: A public park

CAST: 5 actors, min. 1 girl (+)
+   Girl with Book
    4 Students

STAGE SET: park bench at down center

PROPS: apple, book, video camera, photo camera, pen, notebook, tape measure, trowel, backpack

COSTUMES: All characters wear contemporary middle-school school clothes

LIGHTS UP FULL on GIRL sitting on park bench at down center, eating an apple and reading a book. A few seconds pass, then FOUR STUDENTS enter from right and left: STUDENT #1 carries a video camera, STUDENT #2 carries a tape measure, STUDENT #3 carries a photo camera and backpack, STUDENT #4 carries a notebook and pen. Students spot Girl and approach her, Student #1 videotaping her from behind, Student #2 measuring heighth and width of bench, Student #3 taking snapshots of her from left side, Student #4 standing at right side of Girl and taking notes.

GIRL: What is going on?
STUDENT #4: Don't mind us. We're performing an ethnography.
GIRL: Not with me, you're not! *(Shoos Student #2 away.)* Get away!

(Student #1 continues to videotape, Student #3 continues to take snapshots, Student #2 measures ground next to bench.)

STUDENT #4: It's all right. An ethnography is a descriptive account of a single human lifeway. You *are* human, aren't you?
GIRL: The last time I checked!
STUDENT #1: Can you turn this way when you eat the apple?
GIRL: Shut that thing off!

(Girl jumps up and waves book at Student #1 as Student #1 backs away and lowers video camera; Girl grimaces at Student #3, who lowers camera.)

GIRL: Are you aliens from Planet Whacko?
STUDENT #4: No, we're from Ms. Manterra's "Introduction to Anthropology" class.
STUDENT #1: Our assignment is to go out into the field and study someone.
GIRL: What do you want to study?
STUDENT #2: Your culture.
GIRL: *(Hugs book to her chest.)* Well, it's *my* culture, and you're not getting any! Go get your own!

STUDENT #3: We already have *our* culture. We want to compare it with yours.

GIRL: Well, okay. But why?

STUDENT #4: Because that's what anthropology studies — people and their culture. Anthropology is the study of us.

(Girl muses on this for a moment, then sits on bench and motions for Student #4 to sit on bench also, which Student #4 does.)

GIRL: Tell me more about this culture stuff. When did I get it?

STUDENT #4: The specific elements of culture are always learned. You're not born, say, knowing how to use a fork, or liking one type of music over another or being able to do calculus. All that you learn as you grow up.

GIRL: Who decides what my culture is?

STUDENT #1: A lot of times it's your physical environment. If you live near the North Pole, your culture will be learning how to ice-fish and how to make a sealskin parka and how to build an igloo. Your culture will teach you how to survive in that environment.

STUDENT #2: Your family teaches you culture, too.

GIRL: Oh, like table manners and ballet lessons?

STUDENT #2: That and some major customs and rules society thinks are important, like it's not cool to kill other people. Or disrespect them.

STUDENT #3: And how you're supposed to worship the supernatural.

STUDENT #1: Who it's a good idea for you to marry.

STUDENT #2: What kind of jobs are considered good jobs for you to have, and which aren't.

STUDENT #3: Your family lets you know what moral values are important. And how to present and express yourself to other people in an appropriate manner.

GIRL: But I thought people were basically the same all over the world. I mean, everybody likes music, don't they? And doesn't everybody hate bad fashion? Yuck!

STUDENT #4: True, except it's your culture that shapes your standard of "good" and "bad" in things like music and fashion. Culture is a set of ideas about how to live, and those ideas differ from one society to another.

(Student #1 crosses to Student #2 and stands very close, right in Student #2's face.)

STUDENT #1: Buenas dias, señor (señorita).
STUDENT #2: Buenas dias. Excuse me, but you are standing very close.

(Student #2 backs up from Student #1, who, after a moment, smiles and steps forward to again stand in Student #2's face.)

STUDENT #1: Not really. You are standing very far away. In fact, where I come from in Mexico, you standing so far away would be considered *muy descortés* — very impolite.

(Student #2 backs up from Student #1.)

STUDENT #2: But in my culture — the United States of America — we like to keep a larger distance between people when we talk to them. It feels uncomfortable if you're too close when talking with someone.

(Student #1 steps forward to again stand in Student #2's face.)

STUDENT #1: In my culture, it feels uncomfortable talking to someone unless I am very close.
GIRL: If these two cultures have different ideas about how to conduct a social conversation, why don't they split the difference and accommodate each other by standing a *little* close, but not *too* close?
STUDENT #3: We have a U.N. diplomat in the making!
GIRL: Sounds like an anthropologist is a big snoop, always spying on people and bugging them about their culture.
STUDENT #4: Anthropology does more than just catalog cultural differences. It provides insight on how our culture came to be in the first place. In fact, there are many types of anthropologists.

(Student #2 takes tape measure and begins measuring Girl's head.)

GIRL: What is this person doing to my skull?

STUDENT #1: That's the physical anthropologist. They study our body structure and how it evolved over millions of years.

GIRL: *(Tries to dodge measuring.)* Why don't they study some old dead mummies and fossils?

STUDENT #1: They do. But the physical anthropologist also studies living people to learn how we evolved and how our evolution affected our behavior.

(Student #3 kneels, takes a small trowel out of backpack and begins digging in ground, then photographing the ground.)

GIRL: *(Points to Student #3.)* What's *that* about?

STUDENT #1: That's an archeologist digging on the site of an old military camp ground from the Civil War. They study the artifacts people used in the past.

GIRL: You mean just regular stuff?

STUDENT #1: People didn't keep written records until about five thousand years ago. Archeology is a way of getting objects to tell the story of how people lived in their every day life, whether it's a stone axe or a Star Wars toy.

(Student #4, notebook and pen at ready, sits on bench next to Girl.)

STUDENT #4: I'd like to ask you about your matrilineal descent.

GIRL: *(Recoils.)* I beg your pardon!

STUDENT #1: Calm down. This is the social anthropologist. They study how humans group ourselves and how those groups operate.

GIRL: I'm not a group! I'm an individual!

STUDENT #1: But as an individual you are part of several groups. Your family.

STUDENT #2: Your friends.

STUDENT #3: Your classmates.

STUDENT #4: The members of your soccer team.

STUDENT #1: The kids who cruise the mall on Saturday.

STUDENT #2: Your internet Barbie romance chat group.

GIRL: Hey, how do you know about that?

STUDENT #3: That's what social anthropology studies — relationships among people. And how those relationships shape the way we think and behave.

STUDENT #4: Then there's the linguistic anthropologist who studies human language.

STUDENT #1: Stories and jokes.

STUDENT #2: Folklore and proverbs.

STUDENT #3: Methods of daily communication at work and play.

STUDENT #4: And finally, there's applied anthropology. That's when anthropologists use the information they have about culture to solve real problems of today.

GIRL: Look, I have real problems. I'm a teenager, and nobody likes me!

STUDENT #1-4: Then you should move to Samoa!

GIRL: Huh?

STUDENT #1: In the 1920s an anthropologist named Margaret Mead wrote a book called *Coming of Age in Samoa*. In our modern American culture, being a teenager can be tough — especially for a girl. Mead wanted to find out if that was the case everywhere, so she went to Samoa in the Western Pacific and lived among the people for a long time.

STUDENT #2: She spent most of her time with teenage girls and boys and learned that, in Samoa, young people appeared to be happy and content. Much more so than in quote-unquote civilized cultures.

GIRL: Bummer!

STUDENT #3: Margaret Mead said that we should study how our individual personalities are shaped by our culture.

STUDENT #4: Especially by how we are raised as children.

STUDENT #1: In 1934 anthropologist Ruth Benedict wrote a book called *Patterns of Culture*. She compared the cultures of the Zuni Indians of New Mexico and the Kwakiutl Indians of Vancouver.

GIRL: Didn't all Native Americans have the same culture?

STUDENT #2: Not at all. Besides the many differences in ordinary things like sports, courtship, dancing, hairstyles, marriage, housing, rules about eating, religious beliefs and so on, Benedict discovered that the Zuni and the Kwakiutl cultures each seemed to have a different — well, I guess you'd call it a "center."

STUDENT #3: Benedict said that each human culture was based on a central idea that set the pattern for everything else in the culture.

(Student #2 and Student #3 shake hands, smile, pat each other on the back, nod appreciatively.)

STUDENT #4: The culture of the Zuni Indians stressed cooperation and moderation. The perfect Zuni was someone who was mellow and blended in with the group.

(Student #2 and Student #3 push and shove, growl, bluster, strut aggressively.)

STUDENT #1: But the culture of the Kwakiutl Indians was based on a different pattern. In that culture, the individual was important, and conflict was not a bad thing.

STUDENT #4: Aggression was rewarded, and the Kwakiutl sought wisdom through excess.

GIRL: But every person in a culture isn't exactly the same. Even in the Zuni culture there were probably some aggressive people and probably some mellow folks among the Kwakiutl. At least one or two!

STUDENT #1: You're absolutely right. And in the 1960s, a French anthropologist named Claude Levi-Strauss went a step further. He said it's our dreams and innate urges that create our culture.

STUDENT #4: He said the basic structure of human culture was found in the unconscious mind. And that all our myths and legends are expressions of that structure. If you want to know what a culture really believes, study its mythology.

STUDENT #2: Like Cinderalla. The nice girl gets the prince.

STUDENT #3: Or Jack in the Beanstalk. The clever boy achieves success.

GIRL: So in the end, each person is, like, a sample package of their own culture?

STUDENT #1: Right. That's why the science of anthropology tries to find out as much about each one of *us* as possible.

STUDENT #2: So we can improve our understanding about why we humans do what we do.

STUDENT #3: And help make a world free of war, racism, pollution and all the bad parts of human culture.

GIRL: That's a big job!

STUDENT #4: So you don't mind if we get back to work?

GIRL: Oh no, that's cool.

(Girl resumes reading book and eating apple as Students resume documentating her with video and camera shooting, tape measuring and notetaking.)

GIRL: *(To audience.)* It's nice to know you're part of science — even when you're just eating an apple.

(LIGHTS OUT.)

THE END

Geegaws and Doohickeys:
Indispensable Inventions
and Their Forgotten Inventors

To someone living a century ago, today's world would seem to be awash in miracles — jet airplanes, artificial hearts, talking computers and more. Yet, much of what we now take for granted in our daily life — from antibiotics to crayons — resulted from unplanned experiments or even accidents. Contemporary inventors continue to be a tireless breed, always seeking to create new devices that people can't live without. In recent years U.S. government patents have been issued for such items as a Combined Clothes-Brush, Flask and Drinking-Cup, an Automated Pat-on-the-Back Apparatus, an Antisnoring Device, an Eye Protector for Chickens and a Tooth Pillow for collecting money from the Tooth Fairy. Who knows…maybe in another hundred years, they'll be as indispensable to daily life as the microchip and the skateboard!

RUNNING TIME: 20 minutes

TIME: Late this afternoon

PLACE: School science lab

CAST: 12 actors, min. 7 boys (•), 5 girls (+)

+ Sheila, student
+ Ms. Markley, teacher
• Nicolaus Otto
• Charles Kettering
+ Hedy Lamarr
+ 2 Surfers

• Damon, student
• Mr. Roberts, custodian
• William Lear
• Garrett Morgan
• Dr. George Washington Carver

STAGE SET: mid-sized table at down center with science lab objects — petri dish, beaker, etc.

PROPS: notebook, pen, petri dish, beaker, metal stirring rod, 2 lab goggles, 2 pairs of protective lab gloves, velcro wallet, surfboard, skateboard, peanut

EFFECT: Sound — bubbling of liquid

COSTUMES: Sheila, Damon, Ms. Markley wear standard school attire and Damon has on a denim vest; Mr. Roberts wears a school custodian's uniform; Nicolaus Otto, William Lear, Charles Kettering, Garrett Morgan and Dr. George Washington Carver wear combinations of outfits denoting a professor, auto mechanic and lab scientist; Hedy Lamarr is attired as a 1940s Hollywood film star — long fancy gown, flashy jewelry, sunglasses, a turban hat or long head scarf; Two Surfers wear beach outfits

LIGHTS UP FULL on a school science lab. SHEILA and DAMON stand at lab table at down center. They wear goggles and gloves and are watching the contents of a petri dish; Sheila writes in a notebook as Damon stirs the dish with a metal rod.

SHEILA: Watch out! It's oozing!

DAMON: No, it's okay! Everything's under control!

SHEILA: Damon, I think we should have been a *little* bit more careful...

DAMON: No, Sheila, it's okay, it's good, it's working, it's working, it's, it's—

SHEILA: It's evaporating!

DAMON: Oooh, it *is* getting kind of misty down there.

SHEILA: Maybe the temperature is too hot?

DAMON: Maybe it's too cold?

SHEILA: Uh-oh, there it goes...

DAMON: Going...

SHEILA: Going...

DAMON: *(Removes goggles.)* Gone!

SHEILA: *(Removes goggles.)* Darn! We've been trying this experiment for a whole week!

DAMON: I personally do not enjoy utter and complete failure. It's bad for my digestive system. *(Hiccups.)*

(MS. MARKLEY enters from right and crosses to down center.)

MS. MARKLEY: Hello. How's the experiment going?

SHEILA: Ms. Markley, we've followed every instruction in the book. But we just *can't* make this work!

DAMON: All we get is this weird-looking goo-stuff!

SHEILA: I guess we're just not cut out to be scientists.

MS. MARKLEY: Now, don't be so hasty. The first rule of the experimental process is to be patient. Do you know what the second rule is?

DAMON: To possess a brain?

MS. MARKLEY: To learn from your mistakes.

SHEILA: We sure make a lot of those!

MS. MARKLEY: You're not alone. In fact, many great scientific discoveries have occurred by accident. Damon, look at your shirt.

DAMON: *(Jumps, startled.)* My shirt! Am I on fire? Help!!!

MS. MARKLEY: Calm down. Your shirt has buttons. Plastic buttons, right? In 1867 a printer in New Jersey named John Wesley Hyatt was searching for a substance other than ivory that could be used to make billiard balls. One day he was working in the lab, trying without any luck to get sawdust and paper to bond. Suddenly, he cut his finger.

DAMON: Owww! *(Sticks a finger in his mouth.)*

MS. MARKLEY: Hyatt went to the cupboard to get some collodion. Collodion contains cellulose nitrate, and it was used at the time to treat minor cuts. But the bottle of collodion had spilled, and Hyatt found the shelf covered with a solid sheet of hardened cellulose nitrate.

DAMON: And Hyatt wrapped the sheet around his finger?

MS. MARKLEY: He realized the collodion would work as a binder for the sawdust and paper, much better than glue. And, thus, celluloid — the forerunner of plastic — was born, purely by accident.

(MR. ROBERTS enters from left, carrying a broom and sweeping the floor at down left.)

SHEILA: It's nice of you to cheer us up, Ms. Markley. But I doubt if very many *important* science discoveries were made by accident.

MR. ROBERTS: How about a discovery that saved hundreds of millions of lives — because somebody had a cold?

DAMON: Hi, Mr. Roberts! Are you ready to close the lab?

MR. ROBERTS: Not until you kids get straight about the experimental process. During World War I, a Scottish scientist named Alexander Fleming had served in a battlefield hospital, treating wounded soldiers with antiseptics. But the antiseptics killed the healthy white blood cells faster than they killed the bacteria in the wound. A few years later, Fleming was working in his lab, examining a petri dish of bacteria. He had a bad cold and was sniffling and sneezing. A tear fell from his eye — a single tear — into the dish. The next day, when he examined the bacteria in the dish, he noticed a clear space where his tear had fallen.

MS. MARKLEY: And his conclusion?

MR. ROBERTS: The tear contained a substance — an enzyme called "lysozyme" — that would destroy the bacteria but not harm human tissue.

SHEILA: So that saved millions of lives?

MR. ROBERTS: Not right away. But six years later, Fleming had another happy accident. A piece of mold had fallen into his lab dish, ruining his experiment. Instead of throwing it out, he remembered his previous experience with lysozyme. He studied the mold and realized it was producing something that was killing the bacteria — a substance he was able to synthesize into the drug "penicillin," which has been used ever since to fight deadly bacterial infections worldwide.

DAMON: If we don't get this experiment to work soon, I'll be crying a river of tears!

MR. ROBERTS: Nonsense! You kids should be having fun with science.

SHEILA: But science is *serious*, Mr. Roberts. *I'm* only interested in making discoveries that are going to change the world!

DAMON: And I want to be famous! I want to be the next Thomas Edison, Louis Pasteur, Alexander Graham Bell!

MS. MARKLEY: How about the next Doug Engelbart?

SHEILA & DAMON: Who?

MS. MARKLEY: Every time you use a personal computer, you can thank Doug Engelbart. In the 1960s he designed the computer mouse and the concept of "windows" for computer programs. Bill Gates even compared him to Thomas Edison because of the impact he's had on the computer industry.

MR. ROBERTS: *(To Damon.)* And you can thank Mr. Jacob Davis for that nifty vest you're wearing.

DAMON: Actually, my mom bought it for me at Vest-Mart.

MR. ROBERTS: In 1872 Jacob Davis, a tailor in Nevada, wrote a letter to Levi Strauss, a San Francisco storekeeper who had made a fortune selling supplies to miners during the California Gold Rush.

Davis described a new way of making pants using denim and metal rivets. He convinced Strauss to file a patent with him, and a year later, the first "blue jeans" — or Levis, as they came to be called — were manufactured.

MS. MARKLEY: And the clasp-lockers. Don't forget about Damon's clasp-lockers.

DAMON: My what?

MS. MARKLEY: In 1893, Whitcomb Judson of Chicago got tired of buttoning his shirts and lacing his boots. So invented a device he called a "clasp-locker." We know it today as the "zipper."

MR. ROBERTS: And don't forget about George deMestral and his cockleburs. *(To Damon.)* Bring out your wallet, sonny.

DAMON: Excuse me?

MR. ROBERTS: Come on, bring it out!

DAMON: *(Takes wallet from his back pocket.)* Gee, Mr. Roberts, I spent all my money on lunch, but if you need a couple bucks for a soda—

MR. ROBERTS: Open it up, please.

(Damon opens wallet slowly; SOUND: Velcro coming apart.)

MR. ROBERTS: Close it.

(Damon closes wallet; SOUND: Velcro meshing together.)

MR. ROBERTS: Open again.

DAMON: Is it just me, or am I missing something here? Like, what's going on?

(Damon opens wallet slowly; SOUND: Velcro coming apart.)

MR. ROBERTS: Hear that sound? *(Grabs wallet.)*

SHEILA: Velcro?

MR. ROBERTS: *(Brandishes wallet.)* Cockleburs! In the early 1950s a Swiss scientist named George deMestral was out walking in a field near his home. When he came back, his jacket was covered with cockleburs.

MS. MARKLEY: And he wondered, "What makes cockleburs stick so strongly?"

MR. ROBERTS: He put a cocklebur under a microscope. And he discovered that cockleburs are made up of little hooks, which the cocklebur uses to attach seeds to passing animals.

MS. MARKLEY: It was these tiny hooks that had become caught in the loops in the fabric of deMestral's jacket.

MR. ROBERTS: So deMestral designed a fabric that imitated the hooks and loops — Velcro!

DAMON: That's really amazing, Mr. Roberts. Can I have my wallet back now?

MR. ROBERTS: Certainly. *(Returns wallet.)*

SHEILA: But those are just geegaws and doohickeys. I want to invent things that make a *difference!*

DAMON: And how can you be a real inventor if you're not already a genius?

MS. MARKLEY: Our world is made up of thousands of extraordinary things we take for granted. Behind each one, there stands an individual — just like you and me — who had an open mind and didn't feel silly asking questions. What was the first thing you did after getting up this morning, Sheila?

SHEILA: Ate breakfast. I put a muffin in the microwave.

(PERCY SPENCER enters from left holding a candy bar, stands at down left and addresses audience.)

PERCY SPENCER: My name is Percy Spencer, and I had invented over a hundred electrical items by the time I was fifty years old. Right after the Second World War, I was touring one of my electronics laboratories and stopped for a moment in front of a magnetron. That's the big power tube that drives a radar set. Well, I felt something rather peculiar in my jacket pocket — my candy bar had melted! So, what did I do? I went for some popcorn! That's right. *Unpopped* popcorn, and when I held the bag next to the magnetron, the kernels blew as up white and fluffy as if they'd been roasted over a hot fire! I knew then I had discovered a way to cook large quantities of food in a short time. I called my invention a "radar box," but nowadays folks call it a "microwave oven." Can't beat it for popcorn! *(Exits left.)*

MR. ROBERTS: And then you got in the car to come to school?

(NICOLAUS OTTO enters from right, stands at down right and addresses audience.)

NICOLAUS OTTO: Guten tag. I am Nicolaus Otto of Holzhausen, Germany, and in 1861 I built the first engine powered by gas. It won a gold medal at the Paris Exposition of 1867. Nine years later, I expanded upon Etienne Lenoir's model and built the first internal combustion engine, which you will now find in that wonderful invention, the automobile!

(CHARLES KETTERING enters from left, stands at down left and addresses audience.)

CHARLES KETTERING: Well, Herr Otto did a bangup job of designing the gas-powered engine, but somebody needed to figure out how to turn the dang thing on and off! And that was me, Charles Franklin Kettering of Dayton, Ohio. I invented the first electrical ignition system for automobile engines in 1909. That and the engine-driven generator, which made possible the diesel locomotive, four-wheel brakes and electricity just about anywhere and anytime you need it!

(WILLIAM LEAR enters from right, stands at down right and addresses audience.)

WILLIAM LEAR: When you get that car rolling down the highway, you want something to keep you awake. A little music or news, maybe. My name is William Lear from Hannibal, Missouri, and I invented the first car radio and later on, the eight-track tape player.

(GARRETT MORGAN enters from left, stands at down right and addresses audience.)

GARRETT MORGAN: Of course, before too long, folks were taking their new automobiles just everywhere — clogging up city streets and country lanes and causing all kinds of mischief, even around my home town of Paris, Kentucky. So in 1923 I — that is Garrett Morgan — invented the first traffic signal to slow folks down and clear the intersection.

WILLIAM LEAR: Mr. Morgan is too modest. He also invented the gas mask and safety helmet that firefighters wear. In 1912 he invented the gas mask that saved thousands of soldiers in World War I from poison gas attacks.

NICOLAUS OTTO: In 1916 Herr Morgan used his own mask to rescue workers trapped by a gas explosion in a tunnel under Lake Erie.

CHARLES KETTERING: Garrett Morgan was a scientist and a hero.

GARRETT MORGAN: I just believe in keeping busy, that's all.

(Otto and Lear exit left; Kettering and Morgan exit right.)

DAMON: Well, I rode my skateboard to school. Don't tell me somebody invented that in a science lab!

(TWO SURFERS enter from left, stand at down left and look out into audience; Surfer #1 carries a surfboard, Surfer #2 has a skateboard behind her back.)

SURFER #1: Cowabunga, dude! Let's go surfing!

SURFER #2: Wait, dude. We can't.

SURFER #1: How come, dude?

SURFER #2: Cause, dude, there aren't any waves.

SURFER #1: *(Pause.)* Ohhhh…

SURFER #2: But wait! If we can't surf in the water, why don't we surf on land?

SURFER #2: *(Shows skateboard.)* We'll cut our surfboards in half and put wheels on the bottom. *(Stands on skateboard.)* Then we ride 'em on the sidewalk and street just like real waves!

SURFER #1: And we can practice our surfing moves without actually being in the water!

SURFER #2: Yeh, and it'll grow and spread beyond California and become a sport of its own — the sixth-largest participant sport in the whole world!

SURFER #1: So, dude, like, what do we call this thing?

SURFER #2: I don't know. How about something catchy, like, "surf skates?"

SURFER #1: Yeh!

(Two Surfers exit left; HEDY LAMARR enters from right.)

SHEILA: I guess the invention of the skateboard proves "necessity *is* the mother of invention."

HEDY LAMARR: You said it, sister! I'm Hedy Lamarr, star of the silver screen in the 1930s and '40s, delighted to meet you. When the Second World War broke out, our boys in the armed forces were taking it on the chin from the Axis Powers. I got together with a Hollywood composer friend of mine, George Antheil, and we invented a radio code system the enemy couldn't break, detect or interrupt. It worked like an old-time piano roll, and it worked like a charm. I wouldn't say it won the war for our side, but it didn't hurt any, either! *(Exits right.)*

DAMON: Gee whiz, a movie actress! I thought only scientists could invent things.

MS. MARKLEY: Lillian Moller Gilbreth was a homemaker with twelve children. Did she have her hands full! She invented the electric food mixer and the trash can with step-on lid-opener to make life easier around the home.

MR. ROBERTS: Ann Moore was a Peace Corps worker in Africa in the early 1960s. She noticed that the slings native women used to carry their babies let them keep their hands free while keeping the baby safe and comfortable. After Moore returned to America, she and her mother created the "Snugli" baby carrier.

SHEILA: My mom uses that for my baby sister.

DAMON: I wish I could use it now.

MR. ROBERTS: If you want to talk about a single inventor who had a lifelong impact on his world, you're talking about Dr. George Washington Carver of Tuskegee Institute, Alabama.

(DR. GEORGE WASHINGTON CARVER enters from right, stands at down right and looks out into audience.)

DR. GEORGE WASHINGTON CARVER: In the late 1800s the American South was very, very poor. Most of our people were small farmers who lived off the land — or tried to. It was clear to me, as an agricultural chemist, that we needed new ways of growing crops and new ways of using the crops we grew. *(Takes a peanut from his jacket pocket and holds it up.)* And it all started with this little fellow right here — the peanut.

MR. ROBERTS: Dr. Carver developed the method of crop planting called "rotation," which advised farmers to plant different crops in their field each year. That way the nutrients in the soil wouldn't be depleted. Dr. Carver discovered that the peanut was especially good at enriching poor soil.

MS. MARKLEY: Farmers began producing large quantities of peanuts, which up till then had been regarded as a weed and a nuisance. Dr. Carver developed over three hundred uses for the peanut, from printers' ink to cooking oil.

DR. GEORGE WASHINGTON CARVER: Adhesives, axle grease, bleach, creosote…

MR. ROBERTS: Fuel briquettes, instant coffee, insulating board, meat tenderizer…

DR. GEORGE WASHINGTON CARVER: Metal polish, milk flakes, paper, paint and rubbing oil…

MS. MARKLEY: Soil conditioner, shampoo, shoe polish and shaving cream…

DR. GEORGE WASHINGTON CARVER: Synthetic marble and rubber…

MR. ROBERTS: Talcum powder and vanishing cream…

DR. GEORGE WASHINGTON CARVER: Wood stains and wood filler...

MS. MARKLEY: Laundry soap and laxatives...

MR. ROBERTS: And don't forget Worcestershire Sauce!

MS. MARKLEY: By the time of his death in 1943, Dr. Carver had created hundreds of products from the peanut, sweet potato, soybean and pecan, as well as more than five hundred new dyes and pigments from other plants. His inventions — drawn mostly from the simple bounty of nature — were proof that even something as small as a peanut could make such a big difference in so many lives.

(DR. GEORGE WASHINGTON CARVER exits right.)

DAMON: Gee, Ms. Markley, I guess we never realized all the different ways you can invent something.

MS. MARKLEY: The important thing is never to give up. And if you make a mistake, don't just throw the experiment out. It might lead you in a new direction — and a whole new world of wonder. See you tomorrow in class! *(Exits right.)*

SHEILA & DAMON: Good night, Ms. Markley!

MR. ROBERTS: Give it another go before you quit for the day. I'll check back in a while. *(Exits left.)*

(Damon idly stirs dish with rod as Sheila writes in her notebook; suddenly Damon reacts and pulls rod out of dish; they both back up a step and stare fixedly into the dish. SOUND: bubbling of liquid, crescendoing under dialogue.)

SHEILA: What is it?

DAMON: I don't know. Do you think it could be alive?

SHEILA: It's moving, isn't it?

DAMON: I think it's growing.

SHEILA: Did you say "glowing?"

DAMON: That, too.

SHEILA: Are those...eyes?

DAMON: I'm not sure. When was the last time something in a lab dish winked at you?

SHEILA: Should we call somebody?

DAMON: What would George Washington Carver do?

SHEILA: Or Alexander Fleming?

DAMON: Or Garrett Morgan?

SHEILA: They'd stand their ground and face the challenge head-on.

DAMON: Firm in the face of the unknown.

SHEILA: Undeterred by fear or failure.

(Pause as bubbling sound increases.)

DAMON: And *then* they'd run for help.

SHEILA: Yes!

DAMON: Okay, first things first. Let's plant this puppy!

(With great resolve, Sheila and Damon put their goggles back in place over their eyes and step forward to the table.)

SHEILA: If I have but one life, let me give it for science!

DAMON: At least until the weekend!

(LIGHTS OUT.)

THE END

The Author

L.E. McCULLOUGH, PH.D. is a playwright, composer and ethnomusicologist whose studies in music and folklore have spanned cultures throughout the world. Dr. McCullough is the Administrative Director of the Humanities Theatre Group at Indiana University-Purdue University at Indianapolis. Winner of the 1995 Playwrights Preview Productions Emerging Playwright Award for his stage play *Blues for Miss Buttercup,* he is the author of *The Complete Irish Tinwhistle Tutor, Favorite Irish Session Tunes* and *St. Patrick Was a Cajun,* three highly acclaimed music instruction books, and has performed on the soundtracks for the PBS specials *The West, Lewis and Clark* and *Not for Ourselves Alone: The Story of Elizabeth Cady Stanton and Susan B. Anthony.* Since 1991 Dr. McCullough has received 40 awards in 31 national literary competitions and had 178 poem and short story publications in 90 North American literary journals. He is a member of The Dramatists Guild, American Conference for Irish Studies, Southeastern Theatre Conference and National Middle School Association. His books for Smith and Kraus include: *Plays of the Songs of Christmas, Stories of the Songs of Christmas, Ice Babies in Oz: Original Character Monologues, Plays of America from American Folklore, Vol. 1 & 2, Plays of the Wild West, Vol. 1 & 2, Plays from Fairy Tales, Plays from Mythology, Plays of People at Work* and *Anyone Can Produce Plays with Kids.*